Beyond the C.

Elevated Meat Dishes for Epicurean Enthusiasts

By

Sheila R. Shillings

BEEF.

How to choose and cook Beef—Sirloin—Rib—Rump—Fillet—Heart—Baked Beef
—Potted—Stew—A la Daube—Al-a mode—Braised—Minced—Collops—
Boullie—To Collar—Steaks—Tongue—Tripe, &c. &c.

No.

1. Sirloin.
2. Rump.
3. Edge bone.
4. Buttock, or Round,
5. Mouse Buttock.
6. Veiny Piece.
7. Thick Flank.
8. Thin Flank.
9. Leg.
10. Fore Rib. (Five Ribs.)
11. Middle Rib. (Four Ribs.)
12. Chuck Rib. (Three Ribs.)
13. Shoulder, or Leg of Mutton Piece
14. Brisket.
15. Clod.
16. Neck.
17. Shin.
18. Cheek.

To Choose Beef—If young and freshly killed, the lean of ox-beef will be smoothly grained, and of a fine, healthy, carnation-red, the fat rather white than yellow, and the suet white and firm. Heifer-beef is more closely grained, and rather less bright of color, the bones are considerably smaller, and the fat of a purer white.

In choice and well-fed beef, the lean will be found inter-grained with fat: very lean meat is always of an inferior quality.

The ribs, the sirloin, and the rump, are the proper joints to roasting. The round, or buttock, the edge-bone, the second round, or mouse-buttock, the shin, the brisket, the shoulder, of leg of mutton piece, and the clod may be boiled or stewed. The neck is generally used for soup or gravy; and the thin flank for collaring. The best steaks are cut from the middle of the rump; the next best from the veiny piece, or from the chuck-rib. The inside of the sirloin, commonly used for the purpose in France, makes by far the most delicate steaks: but though *exceedingly* tender, they are considered by epicures to be wanting in flavor.

The finest part of the sirloin is the chump-end, which contains the larger portion of the fillet: of the ribs, the middle ones are those generally preferred by experienced house-keepers.

———

Keeping Meat.—As soon as the meat is brought in, it should be wiped dry and examined, and the fly-blown parts, if any, should be cut off. This should be attended to daily, else, when dressed, the outer slices are liable to have a musty flavor.

———

Sirloin of Beef to Roast.—The sirloin is usually hung a few days, to make it eat short and tender, therefore, before you dress it, you should wash the meat in cold water, wipe it with a clean cloth; when you have made it nice and clean, hang it carefully down to the fire, so that it may turn round evenly; a piece of writing-paper, well buttered, must be tied on with a string, or skewered on with very small skewers, over the fat side till the meat is about three parts done, to prevent the fat from burning. A good durable fire having been made up, the meat should be so hung down, that the thickest part of the joint will get the strongest part of the fire, but not too near at first, or it will get scorched on the outside, before it is warmed through. Put into the dripping-pan a pint of water, or clean dripping, and begin to baste the meat immediately it is warmed, and continue to baste it every quarter of an hour, till about half an hour before it is done. Then take the meat back from the fire; clean out all grit that has fallen into the dripping-pan; take off the paper that covered the fat, stir the fire, if necessary, that it may burn fierce and clear, baste the meat well; sprinkle a little salt all over the joint, and dredge it well with flour. Put it to the fire again, and let it roast till it is done, and the outside is nicely browned and frothed; observing not to baste it for a full quarter of an hour after flouring it.

A sirloin weighing ten pounds, that has been kept a proper time, will take two hours and a half to roast it. Rather more time must be allowed in cold than in hot weather. About twenty minutes to the pound, is a safe rule.

Ribs of Beef.—Ribs of Beef should also be kept hanging a few days to become short and tender, therefore wipe and make it nice and clean before you hang it to the fire, as directed for the sirloin; there are sometimes two and sometimes three ribs to a joint; and it must be cooked the same way as the sirloin; only they are best done, and eat nicest, if they are hung to roast the thick part upwards, at first, till they are full half done, or rather longer; but take care to hang it so that the thick part gets the most of the fire; and be sure to tie well buttered paper over the fat part, as directed for the sirloin. Less time, however, will be required for roasting the ribs than the sirloin, because the joint is thinner. From three hours to three hours and a half, may be allowed for ribs of beef weighing fifteen or sixteen pounds; giving a little more time if a thick joint, and a little less if a thin one. When the joint is a little more than half done, you must hang it the other way up wards, baste it, sprinkle it with salt, and dredge it very slightly with flour; but sprinkle it with salt, and dredge it well again with flour, about half an hour before you take it up, first taking off the paper which covers the fat, as directed for the sirloin.

Rump of Beef.—This is one of the most juicy of all the joints of beef, but is more frequently stewed than roasted. As it is too large to serve whole, generally, cut as much from the chump end to roast as will make a handsome dish. Manage it as the sirloin. When boned and rolled into the form of a fillet of veal, it requires more time.

Gravy Sauce for Roast Beef.—When beef is of a good quality, and roasted with care, the gravy which flows from it is the best sauce for the meat. Clear it of the fat and sediment, add a little salt, and if too thin, a dust of browned flour, and boil it up. To the gravy of veal, a little butter may be added.

Pickles or grated horse-radish should always be served with roast beef—with catsup and mustard in the castor. The vegetables most in favor are potatoes, plain boiled or mashed—turnips, beets, and boiled spinach.

———

To Roast a fillet of Beef.—Raise the fillet from the inside of the sirloin, or from part of it, with a sharp knife; leave the fat on, trim off the skin, lard it through, or all over, or roast it quite plain; baste it with butter, and send it very hot to table, with tomato sauce, or sauce piquante, or eschalot sauce, in a tureen. It is sometimes served with brown gravy or currant jelly: it should then be garnished with forcemeat-balls. If not very large, an hour and a quarter will roast it well with a brisk fire.

Obs. The remainder of the joint may be boned, rolled, and roasted or braised; or made into meat cakes; or served as a miniature round of beef.

———

To Roast Beef Heart.—Wash it well, and clean all the blood carefully from the pipes; parboil it ten or fifteen minutes in boiling water; drip the water from it; put in a stuffing which has been made of bread crumbs, minced suet or butter, sweet marjorum, lemon thyme, and parsley, seasoned with salt, pepper, and nutmeg. Put it down to roast while hot, baste it well with butter, froth it up, and serve it with melted butter and vinegar; or with gravy in the dish, and currant jelly in a sauce tureen. To roast, allow 20 minutes to a pound.

———

To dress the Inside of a Cold Sirloin of Beef.—Cut off the meat, with a little of the fat, into strips 3 inches long and half an inch thick; season with pepper and salt, dredge them with flour, and fry them brown in butter; then simmer them in a rich brown gravy; add of mushroom catsup, onion, and shalot vinegar a table-spoonful each. Garnished with fried parsley.

———

Baked Beef.—A rump of 20 to 25 lbs. weight. Take 2 oz. each of pepper and allspice, 1 oz. of pounded cloves, and the same quantity of mace; rub this all over the joint, which should be hung up for a fortnight or 3 weeks, according to the weather—taking care to keep it dry, and to occasionally renew the seasoning.

When ready for baking, wash off the spice with port wine or warm vinegar and water, and lard the rump throughout, by inserting large lardoons in different parts of the meat. Then put a large quantity of suet, shred fine, both under and over it, and cover it with coarse flour and water paste, between which and the suet you may put a few bay-leaves or some sweet-herbs. If eaten hot, the dough, bay-leaves, and suet must all be taken off; the joint basted, sprinkled with a little salt and flour, over which a salamander should be passed; and served up with strong gravy or brown sauce. If cold, leave on the dough till wanted.

It should be baked in a moderately-heated oven, and will take according to the size, from 6 to 8 hours' baking

———

A Round of Beef may be dressed in the same manner; but the bone should in that case be taken out, and the hole filled up with forcemeat. The flap should be filled in like manner, skewered, and tightly bound round with linen or strong tape, in which case the dough and the larding may be omitted, though the latter will be found an improvement. It should be always left until cold.

———

Brisket.—Take all the bones out of 8 lbs of brisket of beef, make holes in it about an inch asunder, and fill one with fat bacon, a second with parsley, a third with oysters, and so on, each being chopped and seasoned with pepper, salt, nutmeg, and cloves. When completely stuffed, lay it in a pan, dredge it well with flour, pour upon it a half pint of water, and the same of broth. Bake it 3 hours, and then skim off the fat; put the meat into a dish, strain the gravy over, and garnish with pickles.

Any piece of fresh beef, even of the coarsest pieces, may be dressed in this manner, or baked before the fire in a Dutch oven with button onions, the meat being previously rubbed over with oil. It is a common mode in Portugal and Spain.

———

Potted Beef.—Rub two pounds of lean beef with salt and saltpetre, and let it lie for two days; then dry the meat, season it with black pepper, and put it into a small pan with half a pound of butter: cover it with paste, and bake slowly for about four hours. When cold, pick out the stringy pieces. cut up the lean, and beat it in a mortar with a quarter of a pound of fresh butter just warmed, and a little of the gravy, seasoning with pounded mace, allspice, and pepper, to taste: when beaten to a very smooth paste, put the beef closely into small pots, and pour on it clarified butter. If to be kept a long time, tie it over with bladder, and set it in a dry place.

Or, the beef may be baked without being previously salted in which case, salt should be added in beating it.

Or, beat in a mortar with butter, pepper, salt, and nutmeg, beef that has been dressed, either boiled or roasted.

———

To Stew Beef.—It should be put down in a pot with just sufficient cold water to cover the meat, and closely covered. After boiling 3 or 4 hours, according to the size of the piece, cut in small pieces, not larger than dice, 2 or 3 carrots and heads of celery, with a little sweet herbs, and put them into the pot along with peppercorns, mace, and a couple of large onions stuck full of cloves, and let it then simmer by the side of the fire for 2 or 3 hours, taking care to skim off any grease that may appear on the top.

By this time the meat will probably be tender enough; when take out the whole onions, mince them, and fry them in butter, to be mixed in the gravy made by the meat, which season with salt and cayenne, or chili vinegar, to which add some mushroom or walnut ketchup. Thicken the gravy with a little flour, and brown it, if necessary, with a spoonful of sugar burnt soft; which, besides imparting its color, adds an agreeable flavor. Such is the most simple mode; but the sauce may be much improved by a glass or two of port wine and a spoonful of curry powder: if the odor of garlic be not objected to, a clove boiled in the stew will be found to give it a fine flavor. Garnish with vegetables.

A small piece of beef—say of 4 lbs.—will take the time mentioned; but the large joints will require full double that time; and should be put to stew overnight, adding the vegetables in the morning.

———

To stew a Rump of Beef.—Wash it with care, and season it well with pepper, salt, ground allspice, mace, and cloves; then tie it up, and put it into a pot, upon twigs or wooden skewers, to prevent the meat from sticking; add to it three large onions sliced, two turnips, three carrots, a shalot, some celery, and a handful of sweet herbs. Cover the meat with boiling water, add beef or mutton shankbones, and simmer the whole till tender, or about four hours. Then strain the gravy, take off the fat, and add from half a pint to a pint of port wine or sherry, or the juice of a fresh lemon, and a table-spoonful of mushroom ketchup; thicken it, simmer for half an hour, and then pour it over the beef. Garnish with carrots and turnips.

Beef and Sauer Kraut.—Boil about six pounds of beef for five minutes; then put it into a stewpan, cover it with sauer kraut, and add a pint of weak gravy; stew gently for four hours, and serve in a deep dish.

Fricandeau of Beef.—Lard a piece of lean beef, with bacon seasoned with pepper, cloves, mace, and allspice. Put it into a stewpan, with a pint of broth, or beef gravy, a glass of sherry, a bundle of parsley, and of sweet herbs, a clove of garlic, and a shalot or two. When the meat is tender, cover it closely; skim the sauce, strain it, and boil till it is reduced to a glaze; then glaze the larded side, and serve the fricandeau on tomato sauce to make which, see *Sauces.*

A Family Stew of Beef.—Take any piece of beef good for stewing, cut it into small pieces, slice 2 or 3 large onions, and put them into the stewpan with 2 ounces of butter or good beef-dripping. When melted, dredge in some flour, add the meat also dredged with flour, and enough water to keep it from burning. When the gravy has drawn, fill up with boiling water, let it come to a boil gently, skim the pot well, then add a spoonful of mixed spices, and a bay-leaf or two; set the pan by the side of the fire to stew slowly for a couple of hours, 6 lbs. of meat will take 3 hours. This dish may be thickened like Irish stew, with potatoes, or it may be served with the addition of chopped vegetables of all kinds, previously fried.

Beef à la Daube.—Lard well a round of beef and put it in a stew-pan; take the meat from a shin of beef, or any other fresh meat, and cut it in small slices; cut also a few slices of bacon, and place them around and over the beef with slices of carrot, and onion; season with pepper, salt, and thyme. Cover the whole with water, and let it stew very slowly from 4 to 6 hours till perfectly done; then take out the round and let it cook.

To make the jelly, take all the meat from the stew-pan, and strain the broth through a sieve: skim the fat from the top very carefully. Put it over the fire, with a few grains of pepper, and let it simmer slowly; beat the whites of 4 eggs in a cup of water and stir them in; let it remain on the fire simmering slowly for about 15 or 20 minutes: strain the jelly, and when it is cool garnish the beef with it.

This dish should be prepared the day before it is wanted. The stew-pan should not be too large.

Beef à la Mode.—Take a round of fresh beef and cut deep slits in it; grate a loaf of stale bread, mix with it thyme, sweet marjoram, one onion chopped fine, cayenne pepper, salt, cloves, mace to your taste—an egg boiled hard and chopped fine, and one-quarter of a pound of butter: stuff the beef, and brown it with a sufficient quantity of butter. When brown, add water enough to stew it. When nearly done, add 1 glass of wine, or the juice of a sweet orange. It will take 4 or 5 hours to stew.

Beef Olives.—Cut cold under-done beef, in slices half an inch thick, and 4 inches square: cover them with crumbs of bread, a little fat, finely shred shalot, pepper, and salt. Roll the slices up, and fasten them with a small skewer; then put them into a stew-pan, with the gravy of the joint, and a little water, and stew them till tender. Serve with beef gravy.

Fillet of Beef.—Cut the inside of a sirloin or rump in slices half an inch thick; trim them neatly; melt a little butter in a frying pan; season the fillets; fry them lightly; serve with tomato sauce, sorrel, anchovy butter, or gherkin sauce.

Fillet of Beef Braised.—Take the inside of a sirloin of beef, stuffed or plain, but rolled together so as to bring the fat into the centre. Then strew the bottom of the stew-pan with a few slices of ham, in which a small quantity of gravy has been put, just to prevent the bottom of the pan from burning; and on this place the meat, covering it with chopped carrots, celery, button onions, and a pickled chili, together with a sliced gherkin, sweet herbs, salt, mace, and a little allspice, and simmer until tender, then brown it before the fire or with a salamander, skim and season the sauce, and send the meat, sauce, and vegetables, up in the same dish.

Beef Kidney.—Trim, and cut the kidney into slices; season them with salt and pepper, and dredge them well with flour; fry them on both sides, and when they are done through, lift them out, empty the pan, and make a gravy for them with a small slice of butter, a dessert-spoonful of flour, pepper and salt, and a cup of boiling water; shake these round, and give them a minute's simmering: add a little mushroom catsup, lemon juice, eschalot vinegar, or any store sauce that will give a good flavor. Minced herbs are to many tastes an improvement to this dish, to which a small quantity of onion shred fine can be added when it is liked. 6 to 9 minutes.

———

To Mince Beef.—Shred the under-done part fine, with some of the fat; put into a small stew-pan some onion or shalot (a very little will do), a little water, pepper, and salt; boil it till the onion is quite soft; then put some of the gravy of the meat to it, and the mince. A few minutes will dress it, but do not let it boil. Have a small hot dish with sippets (small pieces) of bread ready, and pour the mince into it, but first mix a large spoonful of vinegar with it. If shalot vinegar is used, there will be no need of the onion nor the raw shalot.

———

Savory Minced Collops.—Make a little brown thickening with about an ounce and a half of butter, and a dessert-spoonful of flour; when it begins to be colored, shake lightly into it a large teaspoonful of finely shred parsley or mixed savory herbs, two-thirds as much of salt, and half the quantity of pepper. Keep these stirred over a gentle fire until the thickening is of a deep yellow brown; then add a pound of rump steak, finely minced, and keep it well separated with a fork until it is quite hot; next pour to it gradually half a cupful of boiling water, and stew the collops very gently for ten minutes. Before they are served, stir to them a little catsup, Chili vinegar, or lemon juice: a small quantity of minced onion, eschalot, or a *particle* of garlic, may be added at first to the thickening when the flavor is not objected to.

Breslaw of Beef; (good.) — Trim the brown edges from half a pound of under-dressed roast beef, shred it small, and mix it with 4 oz. of fine bread crumbs, a teaspoonful of minced parsley, and two-thirds as much of thyme, 2 oz. of butter broken small, half a cupful of gravy or cream, a high seasoning of pepper and cayenne, and mace, or nutmeg, a small tea-spoonful of salt, and 3 large eggs, well beaten. Melt a little butter in a pie dish, pour in the beef, and bake it half an hour; turn it out, and send it to table with brown gravy in a tureen. When cream or gravy is not at hand, an additional egg or two, and rather more butter, must be used. We think that grated lemon-rind improves the breslaw.

———

Bouilli.—The rump of beef is best for this purpose, as the meat is to be served up in a separate dish, and will make a finely-flavored sort of soup. Take as much of it as may be thought necessary; but for a small party, say from 4 to 6 lbs., along with 2 or 3 large roasted onions, in one of which some cloves may be stuck, and a moderate quantity of whole pepper, with a bunch of sweet herbs; to which an anchovy may be added: put it in a stewpan, covered with rather more than a pint of cold water to every pound of meat; and let it simmer by the side of the fire for 4 or 5 hours, or until it has become quite tender; then take out the herbs and onions, and add carrots, turnips, and celery, either cut into small squares or sliced, and let the whole boil until sufficiently stewed, and ready for the table.

The soup should then be strained off, and served separately, leaving only so much as may be necessary for making sauce for the vegetables. The sauce should be a little thickened, and seasoned to the palate; if a clove of garlic, or a tea-spoonful of garlic and chili vinegar, be added, it will improve the flavor. In Ireland it is not uncommon to send up the bouilli smothered in onion-sauce, the other vegetables being either not used, or brought up in the soup; in France it is very usual to dress cabbage and sausages as an accompaniment to the bouilli; but, in England, it is more customary to serve it up with the vegetable-sauce as above stated. Cucumbers cut into dice and stewed, with a spoonful of chili vinegar added, are served at most of the German hotels. The meat, if gently stewed until quite tender, without being boiled to rags, will be found excellent, and the whole an admirable dish.

Another Boulli.—Take a handsome piece of brisket of 10 lbs. weight; put it over the fire with a small quantity of water until the gravy is out; add a very large bunch of parsley, pepper, salt, and an onion. When the gravy is drawn, add 2 gallous of boiling water, and let it stew until perfectly tender; chop the parsley, and lay it on the top of the meat, thicken the gravy with vegetables, and serve it up.

Or:—Take about 9 lbs. of the beef, tie it tightly with a tape, and put it into a stewpan with just sufficient water to cover it: add onions, celery, a little parsley, and spice: allow it to boil gently, and, when about half done, add a large anchovy. Cut a small quantity of carrots, greens, and capers very fine, mix them with a part of the soup; let them stew till tender, and then serve them with the beef, laying part on the top and the rest round; or, served up separately, and smothered in onion sauce.

The tops of the long ribs make good bouilli, simmered in a small quantity of water, and served on a bed of red cabbage, stewed separately, and flavored with a glass of vinegar. It also eats excellently, if, when simply boiled, it is served up smothered with onion sauce.

———

Ribs of beef, though rarely dressed *en bouilli,* are yet most excellent when so prepared. Take the middle of the flat ribs of beef, stew it until the meat is tender and the bones will come out, employing as small a quantity of water as will cover the meat, and a bundle of sweet herbs. Let it stand until it is cold, remove the fat, add to the gravy, carrots, turnips, and celery, cut in dice, and a dozen or two of small silver onions; warm up the beef in it, and send it to table.

————

Bouilli with Tomatoes.—Take a rump of beef, and have the bone taken out *by the butcher:* put it in water just enough to cover it; and let it boil slowly until it is tender. Then season it to your taste with salt, pepper, mace, and cloves, pounded fine. Dress tomatoes as a vegetable, strain them, pour them over the beef after it is dished, and let them mix with the gravy. It is important to boil the beef a *long time and slowly.*

————

To collar Beef.—Salt the thin end of the flank daily for a week with salt and saltpetre; then take out all bone, gristle, and inside skin, and cover it with this seasoning, cut finely: a handful of sage, the same of parsley, some thyme, marjoram, and pennyroyal, pepper, and allspice. Roll up the meat in a cloth, tie it very tight, and boil it gently for about eight hours. Then take it up, do not untie it, but put on it a heavy weight to make the collar oval. A piece of the breast of veal, rolled in with the beef, is an improvement.

————

To boil a Rump of Beef.—Mix some common salt, a little saltpetre, some parsley, thyme, marjoram, green onions, and pepper; rub all well into the meat, and let it lie 3 or 4 days; then put it into a pot, and cover it with water; add some celery with 2 or 3 sliced carrots, and some small whole onions. Let it simmer gently 3 or 4 hours, according to the size, skimming it carefully, and serve with vegetables.

The other joints that are usually salted and boiled are the *round,* the *aitch-bone* and the *brisket.*

————

Boiled Scarlet Beef.—Take a brisket or thin flank of beef, and rub it well all over with equal quantities of common and bay salt, and an ounce of saltpetre; let it remain for 4 or 5 days in an earthen pan, when it will become red; it should be turned once every day. Boil it gently for 4 hours, and serve it hot, with savoys or any kind of greens; or leave it to get cold, and press it with a heavy weight.

———

Sauce Piquante for Boiled Beef.—Brown in a pan a little butter and flour, add to it half pint of the soup from the beef, 1 carrot, 2 onions, and 1 clove of garlic chopped fine. Let it stew for about 15 minutes. Then add a pickled cucumber chopped fine, and a table-spoonful of vinegar. Let the whole stew for a few minutes, and pour it over the beef when served.

———

To broil Beef Steaks.—The steaks should be from half to three-quarters of an inch thick, equally sliced, and freshly cut from the middle of a well kept, finely grained, and tender rump of beef. They should be neatly trimmed, and once or twice divided, if very large. The fire must be strong and clear. The bars of the gridiron should be thin, and not very close together. When they are thoroughly heated, without being sufficiently burning to scorch the meat, wipe and rub them with fresh mutton suet; next pepper the steaks slightly, but never season them with salt before they are dressed; lay them on the gridiron, and when done on one side, turn them on the other, being careful to catch, in the dish in which they are to be sent to table, any gravy which may threaten to drain from them when they are moved. Let them be served the *instant* they are taken from the fire; and have ready at the moment, dish, cover, and plates, as hot as they can be. From 8 to 10 minutes will be sufficient to broil steaks for the generality of eaters, and more than enough for those who like them but partially done.

Genuine amateurs seldom take prepared sauce or gravy with their steaks, as they consider the natural juices of the meat sufficient. When any accompaniment to them is desired, a small quantity of choice mushroom catsup may be warmed in the dish that is heated to receive them; and which, when the not very refined flavor of a raw eschalot is liked, as it is by some eaters, may previously be rubbed with one, of which the large end has been cut off. A thin slice or two of fresh butter is sometimes laid under the steaks, where it soon melts and mingles with the gravy which flows from them. The appropriate tureen sauces for broiled beef steaks are onion, tomato, oyster, eschalot, hot horse-radish, and brown cucumber, or mushroom sauce.

Obs. 1.—We have departed a little in this receipt from our previous instructions for broiling, by recommending that the steaks should be turned but *once,* instead of "often," as all great authorities on the subject direct. By trying each method, our readers will be able to decide for themselves upon the preferable one: we can only say, that we have never eaten steaks so excellent as those which have been dressed *exactly* in accordance with the receipt we have just given, and we have taken infinite pains to ascertain the really best mode of preparing this very favorite dish, which so constantly makes its appearance both carelessly cooked and ill served, especially at private tables.

Obs. 2.—It is a good plan to throw a few bits of charcoal on the fire some minutes before the steaks are laid down, as they give forth a strong heat without any smoke.

———

A Spanish Steak.—Take the tenderloin of beef. Have onions cut fine and put into a frying-pan with some boiling butter. When quite soft, draw them to the back part of the pan; and, having seasoned well the beef with pepper and salt, put it in the pan, and rather broil than fry it. When done, put the onions over it, and just as much boiling water as will make a gravy. Let it stew a few minutes.

———

Another Beef Steak, a la Francaise.—Must be cut either from the sirloin or some other prime part of the beef, as *rump* steaks are not known in France. Pour over it 2 large spoonsful of the best Lucca oil, and let it remain all night; then put it and the oil into a frying-pan, with some finely chopped parsley, pepper and salt; fry it until the gravy dries up, and it becomes rather brown. Pour the contents of the pan over the steak as sauce. The steaks are usually garnished with slices of fried potatoes. As butter is not known in the southern states of Europe, oil is there constantly used in lieu of it, and this Parisian practice is borrowed from those countries.

———

Stewed Beef Steaks.—Put the steak into a stew-pan, with a lump of butter, over a slow fire, and turn it until the butter has become a fine white gravy, then pour it into a basin, and put more butter to the steak. When the steak is nicely done, take it out, return all the gravy into the stew-pan, and fry the steak; then add it to the gravy in the stew-pan, with a table-spoonful of wine or of catsup, and a shalot finely sliced; stew it for 10 minutes, and serve it up. Or, fry the steak merely at first, then put it into half a pint of water, an onion sliced, a spoonful of walnut catsup, pepper and salt, cover it close, thicken it with flour and butter, and serve it up very hot.

With Vegetables.—Cut the steak about two and a half inches thick; dredge it with flour, and fry it in butter, of a fine brown. Lay it in a stew-pan, and pour water into the frying-pan; let it boil, and add it to the steak, which is rendered richer by this process; slice in turnips, carrots, celery, and onions, adding pepper, salt, and a little mace. It should be highly seasoned, and sent to table with the surface ornamented with forcemeat balls, carrots and turnips cut into shapes, and sometimes with onion fritters, the vegetables to be put round it.

With Oysters.—Cut the steak rather thick; brown it in a frying pan with butter. Add half a pint of water, an onion sliced, pepper and salt, cover the pan close, and let it stew very slowly for 1 hour; then add a glass of port wine, a little flour, and a dozen or two of oysters, their liquor having been previously strained and put into the stew-pan.

———

Beef Steak Stewed in its own Gravy; (good and wholesome)—Trim all the fat and skin from a rump steak of nearly an inch thick, and divide it once or twice; just dip it into cold water, let it drain for an instant, sprinkle it on both sides with pepper, and then flour it rather thickly; lay it quite flat into a well-tinned iron sauce-pan or stew-pan, which has been rinsed with cold water, of which a tablespoonful should be left in it. Place it over (not upon) a *very* gentle fire, and keep it just simmering from an hour and a half to an hour and three quarters, when, if the meat be good, it will have become perfectly tender. Add salt to it when it first begins to boil, and turn it when rather more than half done. A couple of spoonsful of gravy, half as much catsup, and a slight seasoning of spice, would, to many tastes, improve this dish, of which, however, the great recommendation is its wholesome simplicity, which renders it suitable to the most delicate stomach. A thick mutton cutlet from the middle of the leg is excellent dressed thus. 1½ to 1¾ hour.

———

Beef Steak Pie.—Boil water with a little fine lard, and an equal quantity of fresh dripping, or of butter, but not much of either. While hot, mix this with as much flour as you will want, making the paste as stiff as you can to be smooth, which you will make it by good kneading, and beating it with the rolling-pin. When quite smooth, put a lump into a cloth, or under a pan, to soak till nearly cold.

In raising paste it should be brought to a firm consistence, and of sufficient thickness to hold the meat together; it should therefore not be too rich, and it is easier to be worked if moderately warm than cold. The proper way to raise the crust is by placing the left hand on the lump of paste, and with the right keep working it up the back of the hand, till all be of the proper shape and thickness. When worked into the desired form the meat is then put into the pie, and, when quite full, the lid is put on and fixed to the wall or side; the top being ornamented with some device, also made of paste. Before putting it in the oven glaze it all over with white of egg.

Those who are not a good hand at raising crust, may roll the paste of a proper thickness, and cut out the top of the pie, then a long piece for the sides, then cement the bottom to the sides with egg, bringing the former rather farther out, and pinching both together: put egg between the edges of the paste to make it adhere at the sides. Fill the pie, put on the cover, and pinch it and the side crust together. The same mode of uniting the paste is to be observed if the sides are pressed into a tin form, in which the paste must be baked, after it shall be filled and covered: the tin should be buttered, and carefully taken off when done enough; and as the form usually makes the sides of a lighter color than is proper, the pie should be put into the oven again for quarter of an hour.

Take rump-steaks that have been well hung: beat them gently with a rolling-pin: season with pepper, salt, and a little shalot minced very fine; put the slices in layers with a good piece of fat and a sliced mutton kidney; fill the dish; put some crust on the edge, and about an inch below it, and a cup of water or broth in the dish. Cover with rather a thick crust, and set in a moderate oven. Cut a slit in the paste.

Mutton Pies may be made in the same way.

———

Beef Steak and Oyster Pie.—Prepare the steaks as above, and put them in the pie in alternate layers with oysters. Stew the liquor and beards of the oysters with a blade of mace and a teaspoonful of walnut catsup. Strain it and pour it in the pie, when it is baked. A small pie may be baked in 2 hours.

Veal may be used instead of beef.

———

Beef Tongue.—If it has been dried and smoked before it is dressed, it should be soaked over night, but if only pickled, a few hours will be sufficient. Put it in a pot of cold water over a slow fire for an hour or two, before it comes to a boil. Then let it simmer gently for from 3½ to 4 hours, according to its size; ascertain when it is done by probing it with a skewer. Take the skin off, and before serving surround the root with a paper frill.

An excellent way of preparing Tongues to eat cold.—Season with common salt and saltpetre, brown sugar, a little bay salt, pepper, cloves, mace, and allspice, in fine powder, for a fortnight; then take away the pickle, put the tongue into a small pan, and lay some butter on it; cover it with brown crust, and bake it slowly till so tender that a straw will go through it put it into a tin mould, and press it well, laying in as much fat as possible.

The thin part of tongues, if hung up to dry, grates like hung beef, and also makes a fine addition to the flavor of omelets.

———

To roast a Beef Tongue.—Take a fine large fresh tongue, scald it, and take off the skin; cut it off at the root and trim it neatly; stick a few cloves here and there in it, and put it in a cradle-spit; sprinkle it with salt, and baste it well with butter. Serve it with a good sauce in a sauce-boat, made as follows:—Put into a stew-pan half a pint of port wine, with about half the quantity of well-seasoned gravy; reduce it to one-half; then stir in a good piece of butter and a table-spoonful of flour; add a squeeze of lemon; when the butter is melted and the sauce done, place the tongue in a dish, and serve hot with the sauce poured round. In Spain, the sauce is strongly impregnated with saffron.

———

Fresh Beef Tongue.—Take a green tongue, stick it with cloves, and boil it gently for 3 hours: then brush it over with the yolk of an egg, dredge it well with bread crumbs, and roast it, basting it well with butter. When dished, serve it with a little brown gravy flavored with a glass of wine, and lay slices of currant jelly round it. A pickled tongue, well washed, may be dressed in the same way, and beef-udders also.

A fresh Neat's Tongue and Udder may be roasted together in the manner thus described; but when ready to be dished, instead of currant jelly, put half a pint of gravy into a saucepan, with the juice of a Seville orange, 2 lumps of sugar, a glass of claret, and a piece of butter: toss the whole over the fire, and serve it up with the tongue and udder, garnishing the dish with slices of lemon. The udder should be stuck with cloves, and both should be continually basted.

———

To boil Ox Cheek.—Wash very clean, half a head; let it lie in cold water all night; break the bone in two, taking care not to break the flesh. Put it on in a pot of boiling water, and let it boil from 2 to 3 hours; take out the bone. Serve it with boiled carrots and turnips, or savoys. The liquor the head has been boiled in may be strained and made into Scots barley broth or Scots kale.

———

To stew Ox Cheek.—Clean the head, as before directed, and parboil it; take out the bone; stew it in part of the liquor in which it was boiled, thickened with a piece of butter mixed with flour, and browned. Cut into dice, or into any fancy shape, carrots and turnips, as much, when cut, as will fill a pint basin. Mince 2 or 3 onions, add the vegetables, and season with salt and pepper. Cover the pan closely, and stew it 2 hours. A little before serving, add a glass of port wine or ale.

Many excellent and economical dishes are made of an ox cheek, and it is particularly useful in large families.

———

To dress Kidneys and Skirts.—Wash the kidneys, cut them into slices; take the skin off the skirts, and cut them into small pieces; dust them with flour, and fry them brown in butter. Simmer them an hour in a pint of gravy, with an onion finely minced, some salt and pepper. A little before serving, add a table-spoonful of mushroom catsup. They may be broiled and eaten like a beef steak.

———

To dress Palates and Sweetbreads.—Boil the palates till the black skin can be easily peeled off; parboil the sweetbreads with them; skin and cut the palates into pieces, and if the sweetbreads are large, cut them in two the long way; dust them with flour, and fry them of a light brown, in butter; then stew them in rather more than a pint of the liquor in which they were boiled. Brown a piece of butter with flour; add it, with a little Cayenne, salt, pepper, grated lemon peel, and nutmeg, and a glass of white wine. A little before serving, stirring a spoonful of vinegar, or the squeeze of a lemon.

———

To clean and boil Tripe.—Wash it thoroughly in cold water; then sprinkle fine lime over it, lay it in a tub and cover it with warm water; let it remain about 4 hours, then scrape it with a knife till it is perfectly clean. Wash it in cold water, and lay it in weak salt and water for 4 or 5 days, changing the water every day; then cut it in pieces.

Tripe may be dressed in several ways, but, whatever mode may be employed, it will always be found an improvement to soak it for a whole night in milk. Indeed, if left in the milk until that becomes sour, the acidity thus imparted to it will render it still better.

To boil Tripe.—Put it into hot milk and water, an equal quantity of each; milk may be entirely omitted, or that used in which it may have been soaked; let it boil until quite tender, for 2 or 3 hours. Boil several large onions in 2 waters, so as to diminish their flavor; if Spanish onions can be got, they should be preferred. When quite tender, slice the onions into small flakes, but leave them in that state, and do not mash them into smooth sauce; put the onions into a casserole with milk and butter, so as to make a delicate white sauce, and season it only with a little salt, or a slight grating of nutmeg; then put the tripe, hot from the pot, into a deep dish, and smother it entirely with the sauce. It is usually eaten with pepper and mustard, at the discretion of the guests, Oyster sauce is sometimes used, and much approved.

———

To fry Tripe.—Cut it into bits 3 or 4 inches square; make a batter thicker than for pancakes, of 3 eggs beaten up with flour and milk, a little salt, pepper, and nutmeg; dip in the tripe, and fry it in butter, or fresh dripping, of a light brown color. Serve it garnished with parsley. *Sauce*—melted butter with lemon pickle in it.

———

Sauce for Tripe, Cow-heel, &.—Stir into half a pint of oiled butter, (that is, butter melted and strained,) a table-spoonful of garlic-vinegar, and a tea-spoonful each of made mustard, ground black pepper, and brown sugar.

———

Cow-heels.—Ox-feet, or Cow-heels, are rarely eaten by Americans, but in Europe, and particularly in Great Britain they are always cooked. They contain much nutriment, and may be dressed in the various ways already stated for tripe, with which they are commonly boiled. They are frequently eaten cold, with mustard and vinegar.

Soak them well; boil, and serve in a napkin, with thick melted butter, a large spoonful of vinegar, and a little mustard and salt. Or boil, and then stew them in a brown gravy. Or cut the heel in 4 parts, dip each in egg, flour and fry them in butter. Or fry, and serve with onions fried and put round them: sauce as above.

The water in which they are boiled will make equally good jellies, either relishing or sweet, with that of calves' feet, if duly prepared; and at a far less expense. This jelly gives great additional richness likewise to soups and gravies.

———

To fry Ox-feet, or Cow-heel.—After preparing them as above, cut them into small pieces; have ready some bread finely crumbled, dip the pieces into the yolk of an egg beaten up, and roll them in the bread crumbs mixed with chopped parsley, pepper, and salt; fry them in butter or fresh lard, of a fine brown color.

———

Marrow Bones.—If too long to serve undivided, saw them in two; cover the open end with a lump of paste and a cloth floured and tied close; the paste must be removed before sent to table. Boil 1½ or 2 hours, according to the size; put a ruffle of paper round each, and serve in a napkin, with very hot toast. The marrow is spread upon the toast, and seasoned with pepper and salt.

———

Bubble and Squeak.—Slice under-done cold roast or boiled beef, with fat to fry it a nice light brown; take care that it is not done hard. Mince some cooked cabbage, and fry it with pepper and salt, without burning; lay some in the dish, and lay in the meat, and cover it nicely with the rest, garnishing with fried beet-root, eggs or apples. This is an excellent dish if well made, but very bad if ill done.

Under-done roasted meat may be cut into steaks, and hardened upon the gridiron or in the frying-pan, and served under an oyster, mushroom, onion, or any other ragoût.

———

An Excellent Sandwich.—A thin, tender beefsteak, boiled, and well seasoned with pepper and salt; put quite hot between two slices of bread and butter, and eaten when cold.

VEAL.

To Choose and Cook Veal—Roast Loin—Boiled and Stewed—Fillet, Knuckle— Shoulder—Gohote—Blanquettes—Frican-deau—Rolled Veal—Potted— Minced—Cutlets—Collops—Veal Olives—Neck to Braise—Ragout—Stewed Veal and Peas—Sweetbread—Croquettes—Calf's Head—Dressed many ways —Brains—Feet—Kidney, &c.—Veal Forcemeats.

No.

1. Loin, Best End.
2. Loin, Chump End.
3. Fillet.
4. Hind Knuckle.
5. Fore Knuckle.
6. Neck, Best End.
7. Neck, Scrag End.
8. Blade Bone.
9. Breast, Best End.
10. Breast, Brisket End.

To Choose Veal.—Veal should be fat, finely grained, white, firm, and not overgrown: for when very large it is apt to be coarse and tough. It is more difficult to keep than any other meat except pork, and should never be allowed to acquire the slightest taint before it is dressed, as any approach to putridity renders it equally unwholesome and offensive to the taste. The fillet, the loin, the shoulder, and the best end of the neck, are the parts generally selected for roasting; the breast and knuckle are more usually stewed or boiled. The udder, or firm white fat of the fillet, is much used by French cooks in stead of butter, especially in the composition of their forcemeats: for these, it is first well boiled, then left until quite cold, and afterwards thoroughly pounded before it is mixed with the other ingredients. The head and feet of the calf are valuable articles of food, both for the nutriment which the gelatinous parts of them afford, and for the great variety of modes in which they may be dressed. The kidneys, with the rich fat that surrounds them, and the sweetbreads especially, are well known delicacies; the liver and the heart also are very good eating; and no meat is so generally useful for rich soups and gravies as veal.

Veal, more than any other meat, requires to be wiped with a clean cloth every morning. The kernel should he taken out of the thick fat of the leg, and the udder slightly sprinkled with salt. Cut out the pipe from along the chine-bone of the loin, remove the kernel from under the inside fat, and sprinkle the chine-bone with salt. The pipe and chine-bone should be cut out from the neck, and the inside of the ribs rubbed with salt. From the breast, cut off the loose inside fat, and piece of skirt. The shoulder is rarely kept above a day or two.

———

Roast Loin of Veal.—It is not usual to stuff a loin of veal, but we greatly recommend the practice, as an infinite improvement to the joint. Make the same forcemeat as for the fillet; and insert it between the skin and the flesh just over the ends of the bones. Skewer down the flap, place the joint at a moderate distance from a sound fire, keep it constantly basted, and be especially careful not to allow the kidney fat to burn to prevent this, and to ensure the good appearance of the joint a buttered paper is often fastened round the loin, and removed about half an hour before it is taken from the fire. It is the fashion in some counties to serve *egg-sauce* and brown gravy with roast loin, or breast of veal.

The cook will scarcely need to be told that she must separate the skin from the flank, with a sharp knife, quite from the end, to the place where the forcemeat is to be put, and then skewer the whole very securely. When the veal is not papered, dredge it well with flour soon after it is laid to the fire. 2 to 2½ hours.

———

Boiled Loin of Veal.—If dressed with care and served with good sauces, this, when the meat is small and white, is an excellent dish, and often more acceptable to persons of delicate habit than roast veal. Take from eight to ten pounds of the best end of the loin, leave the kidney in with all its fat, skewer or bind down the flap, lay the meat into cold water, and boil it as *gently as possible* from two hours and a quarter to two and a half, clearing off the scum perfectly, as in dressing the fillet. Send it to table with well-made oyster sauce, or bechamel, or with white sauce well flavored with lemon-juice, and wish parsley, boiled, pressed dry, and finely chopped. 2¼ to 2½ hours.

———

Stewed Loin of Veal.—Take part of a loin of veal, the chump end will do; put into a large, thick, well-tinned iron saucepan, or into a stewpan, about a couple of ounces of butter, and shake it over a moderate fire until it begins to brown; flour the veal well all over, lay it into the saucepan, and when it is of a fine, equal light-brown, pour gradually in veal broth, gravy, or boiling water to nearly half its depth; add a little salt, one or two sliced carrots, a small onion, or more when the flavor is much liked, and a bunch of parsley; stew the veal very softly for an hour or rather more; then turn it, and let it stew for nearly or quite another hour, or longer should it not appear perfectly done. As none of our receipts have been tried with large, coarse veal, the cooking must be regulated by that circumstance, and longer time allowed should the meat be of more than middling size. Dish the joint; skim all the fat from the gravy, and strain it over the meat; or keep the joint hot while it is rapidly reduced to a richer consistency. This is merely a plain family stew.

———

Fillet of Veal Stewed.—Take a fillet of veal, and with a sharp knife make deep incisions in the upper and lower surfaces. Make a rich stuffing of grated bread, sweet herbs, pepper and salt, mixed with the yolk of eggs, and put it into the holes which you have made. Then rub the stuffing thickly all over the meat, with the addition of some ham or bacon cut into very thin slices. Put it into a pot and add enough butter or lard to stew and brown it. It will take about 3 hours to cook. Some persons add the ham, for the stuffing, others leave it out entirely, and do not use the stuffing on the outside. If the ham or bacon is used, it should be very fat and cut very thin.

Fillet of Veal Roasted.—Take out the bone, and fill the space with a fine stuffing of bread crumbs, seasoned with parsley, rather less of marjoram, a little pepper and salt, mixed thoroughly with the yolk and white of an egg or two, according to quantity. A small onion, finely chopped, may be added, and let the fat be skewered quite round; stuff it also well under the skin—as much depends on the quantity and flavor of the stuffing—and send the large side uppermost. Put a paper over the fat; and take care to allow a sufficient time for roasting; put it a good distance from the fire, as the meat is very solid, and must be so thoroughly done as not to leave the least appearance of red gravy; serve it with melted butter poured over, and gravy round. Ham or bacon should be served with it, and fresh cucumbers if in season.

Although considered very indigestible, it is a favorite joint, and easily divided into 3 parts and each dressed separately; that piece known in a "round of beef" as the "silver side" being roasted, and the remaining two stewed in different ways.

In Paris, a *longe de veau* is cut somewhat in the shape of a haunch of mutton, with the fillet and part of the loin joined together.

———

Fillet of Veal Boiled.—Choose a small delicate fillet for this purpose; prepare as for roasting, or stuff it with an oyster forcemeat; bind it round with a tape; after having washed it thoroughly, cover it with milk and water in equal quantities, and let it boil very gently three and a half or four hours, keeping it carefully skimmed. Send it to table with a rich white sauce, or, if stuffed with oysters, a tureen of oyster-sauce; garnish with stewed celery and slices of bacon. A boiled tongue should be served with it.

———

Knuckle of Veal; (en Ragoût.)—Cut in small thick slices the flesh of a knuckle of veal, season it with a little fine salt and white pepper, flour it lightly, and fry it in butter to a pale brown, lay it into a very clean stewpan or saucepan, and just cover it with boiling water; skim it clean, and add to it a faggot of thyme and parsley, the white part of a head of celery, a small quantity of cayenne, and a blade or two of mace. Stew it very softly from an hour and three-quarters, to two hours and a half. Thicken and enrich the gravy, if needful, with rice-flour and mushroom catsup or Harvey's sauce, or with a large teaspoonful of flour, mixed with a slice of butter, a little good store-sauce and a glass of sherry or Madeira. Fried forcemeat balls may be added at pleasure. With an additional quantity of water, or of broth (made with the bones of the joint), a pint and a half of young green peas stewed with the yea for an hour, will give an agreeable variety of this dish.

———

Boiled Knuckle of Veal.—After the joint has been trimmed and well washed, put it into a vessel well adapted to it in size, for if it be very large, so much water will be required that the veal will be deprived of its flavor; it should be well covered with it, and *very gently* boiled until it is perfectly tender in every part, but not so much done as to separate from the bone. Clear off the scum with scrupulous care when the simmering first commences, and throw in a small portion of salt; as this, if sparingly used, will not redden the meat, and will otherwise much improve it. Parsley and butter is usually both poured over, and sent to table with a knuckle of veal, and boiled bacon also should accompany it. From the sinewy nature of this joint, it requires more than the usual time of cooking, a quarter of an hour to the pound not being sufficient for it.

Veal, 6 to 7 lbs: 2 hours or more.

———

Knuckle of Veal with Rice or Green Peas.—Pour over a small knuckle of veal rather more than sufficient water to cover it; bring it slowly to a boil; take off all the scum with great care, throw in a tea-spoonful of salt, and when the joint has simmered for about half an hour, throw in from eight to twelve ounces of well-washed rice, and stew the veal gently for an hour and a half longer, or until both the me at and rice are perfectly tender. A seasoning of cayenne and mace in fine powder with more salt, should it be required, must be added 20 or 30 minutes before they are served. For a superior stew, good veal broth may be substituted for the water.

Veal, 6 lbs.; water, 3 to 4 pints; salt, 1 tea-spoonful; 30 to 40 minutes. Rice, 8 to 12 ozs.: an hour and a half. Seasoning of cayenne, mace, and more salt if needed. A quart or even more of full-grown green peas added to the veal as soon as the scum has been cleared off will make a most excellent stew. It should be well seasoned with white pepper, and the mace should be omitted.

Shoulder of Veal.—Cut off the knuckle for a stew or gravy. Roast the other part with a stuffing; you may lard it. Serve with melted butter.

The blade-bone, with a good deal of meat left on, eats extremely well, when grilled, with mushroom or oyster sauce, or mushroom catsup in butter.

Being a large joint of what is considered rather coarse meat, it is rarely served to any but plain family parties; but, if braised, it makes an excellent dish.

———

Gohote: (a very nice dish.)—Take all the fillet of veal that will chop, and mince it fine. Season it with salt, pepper, a little parsley, and an onion, chopped fine. Add about half a teacup of bread crumbs, a little fat of ham or pork, if not the latter some butter, and 2 eggs. Mix it well with the hands, and make it into one large ball: sprinkle it with bread crumbs, and put several pieces of butter about it. Bake it in 2 hours. Make a good gravy with the scraps and bone, and serve with it.

This may be made of veal that has been once cooked baking it a shorter time.

Blanquettes.—Melt a piece of butter the size of a walnut in a stew-pan; then put in a little thyme, parsley, or any herbs you like the flavor of, and a little onion, all chopped fine, with a pinch of flour. Brown the herbs; add pepper and salt, with a clove or two. Then put in cold or undressed veal, cut in thin slices the size of half a crown; add gravy or broth half a pint, or according to the quantity of meat you want to dress. It should not be too large a dish. Let it stew very gently over a stove; if of dressed meat, 1 hour will be sufficient: add half a teacupful of cream, and stir it well together for a few minutes; then take it up, and before you turn it out have 2 yolks of eggs well beaten, and add to your dish. Give it a few shakes over the fire. It must not boil, or it will curdle.

Or: Cut rabbits, fowl, veal, or lobster, in pieces, steep them (except the veal or fish) in water for half an hour, changing the water. Put some butter in a stew-pan to melt, but do not let it fry; put in the meat with a very little flour, and keep shaking it well; pour in by degrees some broth made of white meat; add a bunch of parsley, an onion, salt, mace, and white pepper. Stew it well a quarter of an hour before it is dished; take out the parsley and onion, and add some raw parsley chopped, and the yolk of an egg and cream beaten together. You must never cease shaking the pan until the blanquette is put over the dish.

———

Veal à la Chartreuse.—Line a copper mould with fat bacon, lay sliced carrots and turnips round the edges, then cover with a forcemeat, and put in a fricassee of veal or fowl. Cover the top of the mould with a paste, steam it an hour, and serve it turned out upon a dish.

———

To Marble Veal.—Boil tender, skin, and cut a dried neat's tongue in thin slices, and beat it as fine as possible, with half a pound of butter and some mace pounded. Have ready some roasted fillet of veal, beaten with butter, and seasoned with white pepper and salt; of this put a thick layer in a large potting-pot, then put in the tongue, in rough, irregular lumps, not to touch each other; fill up the pot with veal, and press it down quite close. Pour clarified butter thick over; keep in a dry, cool place, and serve in thin slices, taking off the butter. Garnish with parsley.

———

Fricandeau of Veal.—Cut a piece about two inches thick from a fillet of veal; shape it like the back of a turtle, high and round in the middle, and thin at the edges, and lard the top and sides very thickly with fat bacon; then put into a stew-pan 4 onions, a carrot, sliced, a bunch of sweet herbs, some allspice, salt, and whole pepper, three blades of mace, and a small piece of lean ham: cover these with slices of fat bacon, and place upon them the veal, which also cover with bacon. Next cover the whole with veal troth, or boiling water, put on the lid, and stew very gently, until the veal is so tender as to be divided with a spoon; then take it up, and quickly boil the gravy, uncovered, to a glaze, which strain, and brush over the fricandeau; to be served upon spinach or endive, tomato, or mushroom-sauce, or upon the remainder of the glaze. A moderately-sized fricandeau will require about three hours and a half stewing.

The lean part of a neck of veal, stewed with the meat of two or three bones in water, will make a plain fricandeau Sweet-breads, larded and prepared as veal, make fine frican deaux, being served in a rich gravy.

Rolled Veal.—The breast is the best for this purpose. Bone a piece of the breast, and lay a forcemeat over it of herbs, bread, an anchovy, a spoonful or two of scraped ham, a very little mace, white pepper, and chopped chives; then roll, bind it up tight, and stew it in water or weak broth with the bones, some carrots, onions, turnips, and a bay-leaf. Let the color be preserved, and serve it in veal gravy, or fricassee sauce.

Potted Veal.—Pound some cold veal, and season it with pepper, salt, and a little mace, in powder; then pound or shred the lean of ham or tongue; put layers of veal and ham, or tongue, alternately into a pot, press them down, put on the top liquid butter, and tie over. This may be cut in slices, or served whole.

Or, the ham or tongue may be put in rough lumps, not to touch each other, so as to marble the veal.

Minced Veal.—Cut, without chopping, cold veal, very finely; grate over it a little lemon peel and nutmeg, and season with pepper and salt; cover the veal with broth, water, or milk, and simmer gently; thicken with flour rubbed in butter, and serve in a deep dish, with sippets of toast bread. A spoonful or two of cream, and a little lemon pickle, are fine additions.

Minced Veal and Oysters.—The most elegant mode of preparing this dish is to mince about a pound of the whitest part of the inside of a cold roast fillet or loin of veal, to heat it without allowing it to boil, in a pint of rich white sauce, or bechamel, and to mix with it at the moment of serving three dozen of small oysters ready bearded, and plumped in their own strained liquor, which is also to be added to the mince; the requisite quantity of salt, cayenne, and mace, should be sprinkled over the veal before it is put into the sauce. Garnish the dish with pale fried sippets of bread, or with *fleurons* of brioche, or of puff-paste. Nearly half a pint of mushrooms minced, and stewed white in a little butter, maybe mixed with the veal instead of the oysters; or, should they be very small, they may be added to it whole: from ten to twenty minutes will be sufficient to make them tender. Balls of delicately fried oyster-forcemeat laid round the dish will give another good variety of it.

Veal minced, 1 lb.; white sauce, 1 pint; oysters, 3 dozens, with their liquor; or mushrooms, half pint, stewed in butter 10 to 12 minutes.

———

Veal Cutlets.—Cutlets should be cut from the fillet, but *chops* are taken from the loin. Some persons have deprecated the practice of beating meat, but it is essentially necessary in veal cutlets, which otherwise, especially if merely fried, are very indigestible. They should be cut about one-quarter or half an inch in thickness, and well beaten; they will then, when fried, taste like sweetbreads, be quite as tender, and nearly as rich. Egg them over, dip in bread crumbs and savoury herbs, fry, and serve with mushroom sauce and fried bacon.

Or:—Prepare as above, and fry them; lay them in a dish, and keep them hot: dredge a little flour, and put a bit of butter into the pan; brown it, then pour a little boiling water into it, and boil quickly; season with pepper, salt, and catsup, and pour it over them.

———

Maintenon Cutlets.—Prepare the cutlets with egg and seasoning, as above, fold them in buttered writing-paper, and broil or fry them. Serve in the paper, and with them, in a boat, sauce as above, sauce piquante, or cucumber sauce.

Lamb and mutton cutlets may be dressed as above.

———

To dress Collops quickly.—Cut them as thin as paper with a very sharp knife, and in small bits. Throw the skin and any odd bits of the veal, into a little water, with a dust of pepper and salt; set them on the fire while you beat the collops; and dip them in a seasoning of herbs, bread, pepper, salt, and a scrape of nutmeg, but first wet them in egg. Then put a bit of butter into a frying-pan, and give the collops a very quick fry; for as they are so thin, 2 minutes will do them on both sides put them into a hot dish before the fire; then strain and thicken the gravy.

Or:—Cut the collops thin; flatten them with a beater; have a large dish, dredge it with flour, and sprinkle a little black pepper over it: as the collops are flattened, lay them in the dish; put a piece of butter in a frying-pan, and, when it is melted and hot, lay in the collops; do them quickly; when lightly browned, dish them up, and serve with a mushroom sauce.

——

Veal Olives.—Cut long thin slices, beat them, lay them on thin slices of fat bacon, and over these a layer of forcemeat, seasoned high with some shred shalot and Cayenne. Roll them tight, about the size of 2 fingers, but not more than 2 or 3 inches long; fasten them round with a small skewer, rub egg over them, and fry them of a light brown. Serve with brown gravy, in which boil some mushrooms, pickled or fresh. Garnish with balls fried.

——

Veal Olives and Collops.—Lay over each other thin slices of veal and fat bacon, and upon them a layer of highly-seasoned forcemeat, with finely shred shalot; roll and skewer them up tightly, egg and crumb them, and fry them brown. Serve them with brown gravy, with pickled or fresh mushrooms; that is, brown mushroom sauce.

——

Neck of Veal.—Take the best end of a neck of veal, cut off the ends of the bones, and turn the flap over; saw off the chine bone, or joint it thoroughly; paper it, and baste it well all the time it is roasting. Larding the fillet or thick part is a great improvement. Or, stew it with rice, small onions, and peppercorns.

Or:—Take the best end of a small neck; cut the bones short, but leave it whole; then put it into a stew-pan just covered with brown gravy; and when it is nearly done, have ready a pint of boiled peas, 3 or 4 cucumbers, and 2 cabbage-lettuces cut into quarters, all stewed in a little good broth; put them to the veal, and let them simmer for 10 minutes. When the veal is in the dish, pour the sauce and vegetables over it, and lay the lettuce round it. This is an excellent summer stew.

——

Neck of Veal à la Braise.—Cut off the ends of the long bones, and saw off the chine-bones: raise the skin of the fillet, lard it very close, and tie it up neatly. Put the scrag end, a little lean bacon or ham, an onion, 2 carrots, 2 heads of celery, and about a glass of Madeira wine, into a stew-pan. Lay on them the neck, add a little water, and stew it 2 hours, or till it is tender, but not too much. Strain off the liquor; mix a little flour and butter in a stew-pan, till brown; stir some of the liquor in, and boil it up; skim it nicely, and squeeze orange or lemon juice into it, and serve with the meat. The bacon should be browned with a salamander and glazed. It may be also served with spinach.

———

Breast of Veal ragoutû.—Cut the breast in two, lengthwise, and divide it into moderately-sized pieces; fry them in butter of a light brown, and put them into a stew-pan with veal broth or boiling water to cover the meat, a sprig of marjoram, thyme, and parsley, tied together, a tea-spoonful of allspice, 2 blades of mace, 2 onions, the peel of a lemon, and salt and pepper to season; cover the whole closely, and stew from 1½ to 2 hours; then strain the gravy, take off the fat, and cover up the veal. Next put a little butter into a small stew-pan, dredge in flour, and gradually add the gravy; boil and skim it; add a glass of white wine, the same of mushroom catsup, and the juice of half a lemon, or, instead of the two latter, a wine-glass of lemon pickle: boil it up and serve in a deep dish with the veal.

———

Stewed Veal and Peas.—Cut into pieces a breast or a neck of veal, and stew it 2 hours, with 2 onions, pepper and salt, and broth or water to cover it; then add 2 quarts of green peas, and a sprig of mint, and stew half an hour longer: thicken, if required, with butter and flour. Dish up the peas, and heap peas in the centre.

Or:—The peas may be stewed separately, thus:—Put a pint and a half into a stew-pan, with a quarter of a pound of butter, a few green onions, and sprigs of parsley; cover them with water, and warm; let them stand a few minutes, then pour off the water, add about an ounce of lean ham; when done, work in a small piece of butter kneaded with flour; keep the peas in motion over the fire until done; season with a tea spoonful of pounded sugar, and pepper and salt.

———

To collar a Breast of Veal.—Remove the bones, thick skin, and gristle, and season the meat with chopped herbs, mace, salt and pepper; then lay between the veal, slices of ham, variegated with hard yolks of eggs, beet-root, and chopped parsley; roll the whole up tightly in a cloth, and tie it. Simmer for some hours, or till tender, in a very little water: when done, lay it on a board with a weight upon it till cold. Then take off the cloth, and pour the liquor over the veal.

———

Sweetbreads (Simply dressed).—In whatever way sweetbreads are dressed, they should first be well soaked in lukewarm water, then thrown into boiling water to *blanch* them, as it is called, and to render them firm. If lifted out after they have boiled from five to ten minutes, according to their size, and laid immediately into fresh spring water to cool, their color will be the better preserved. They may then be gently stewed for three quarters of an hour in veal gravy, which, with the usual additions of cream, lemon, and egg-yolks, may be converted into a fricassee sauce for them when they are done; or they may be lifted from it, *glazed*, and served with good Spanish gravy; or, the glazing being omitted, they may be sauced with sharp sauce. They may also be simply floured, and roasted in a Dutch oven, being often basted with butter, and frequently turned. A full sized sweetbread, after having been blanched, will require quite three quarters of an hour to dress it.

Blanched 5 to 10 minutes. Stewed ¾ hour or more.

———

Sweetbread Cutlets.—Boil the sweetbreads for half an hour in water, or veal broth, and when they are perfectly cold, cut them into slices of equal thickness, brush them with yolks of egg, and dip them into very fine bread-crumbs, seasoned with salt, cayenne, grated lemon-rind, and mace; fry them in butter of a fine light brown, arrange them in a dish, placing them high in the centre, and pour *under* them a gravy made in the pan, thickened with mushroom powder, and flavored with lemon-juice; or, in lieu of this, sauce them with some rich brown gravy, to which a glass of sherry or Madeira has been added.

———

To Broil a Sweetbread.—Parboil it, rub it with butter, and broil it over a slow fire, turn it frequently, and baste it now and then, by putting it upon a plate kept warm by the fire with butter in it.

Veal Croquettes.—Pound, in a marble mortar, cold veal and fowl, with a little suet, some chopped lemon peel, lemon thyme, chives, and parsley. Season with nutmeg, pepper, and salt; mix all well together, and add the yolk of an egg well beaten; roll it into balls, and dip them into an egg beater, up, then sift bread crumbs over them, and fry them in butter.

———

French Croquettes of Sweetbread.—Brown in a little butter and lard 6 sweetbreads; chop them up with a cold tongue that has been parboiled; mix them well and season with a little parsley, an onion, pepper and salt if required. Take the gravy in which the sweetbreads were browned, and when it is cold, break into it 3 eggs; use this to moisten the mincemeat; if not enough add a little other gravy. Take 3 more eggs to roll the croquettes in, with bread crumbs, into the proper shape. Fry them in lard, like fritters; take them up with a ladle with holes in it.

———

To take the Hair from a Calf's Head with the shin on.—It is better to do this before the head is divided; but if only the half of one with the skin on can be procured, it must be managed in the same way. Put it into plenty of water which is on the point of simmering, but which does not positively boil, and let it remain in until it does so, and for five or six minutes afterwards, but at the first full bubble draw it from the fire and let it merely scald; then lift it out, and with a knife that is *not* sharp scrape off the hair as closely and as quickly as possible. The butchers have an instrument on purpose for the operation; but we have had the head look quite as well when done in the manner we have just described, as when it has been sent in ready prepared by them. After the hair is off, the head should be well washed, and if it cannot be cooked the same day, it must be wiped extremely dry before it is hung up; and when it has not been divided, it should be left whole until the time approaches for dressing it. The brain must then be taken out, and both that and the head well soaked and washed with the greatest nicety. When the half head only is scalded, the brain should first be removed. Calves' feet are freed from the hair easily in the same manner.

Boiled Calf's Head.—When the head is dressed with the skin on, which many persons prefer, the ear must be cut off quite close to it; it will require three-quarters of an hour or upwards of additional boiling, and should be served covered with fried crumbs. In either case, first remove the brain, wash the head delicately clean, and soak it for a quarter of an hour; cover it plentifully with cold water, remove the scum as it rises with great care, throw in a little salt, and boil the head gently until it is perfectly tender. In the mean time, wash and soak the brains first in cold and then in warm water, remove the skin or film, boil them in a small saucepan from fourteen to sixteen minutes, according to their size, and when they are done, chop and mix them with eight or ten sage leaves boiled tender, and finely minced, or, if preferred, with parsley boiled instead; warm them in a spoonful or two of melted butter, or white sauce; skin the tongue, trim off the root, and serve it in a small dish with the brains laid round it. Send the head to table very hot, with parsley and butter poured over it, and some more in a tureen. A cheek of bacon, or very delicate pickled pork, and greens, are the usual accompaniments to boiled calf's head.

We have given here the common mode of serving this dish, by some epicures considered the best, and by others, as exceedingly insipid. Tomato sauce sometimes takes the place of the parsley and butter; and rich oyster or Dutch sauce are varieties often substituted for it.

With the skin on, from two and a quarter to two and three quarter hours; without the skin, from 1 hour and a quarter to 1 and three quarters, to boil.

———

To Bake Calf's Head.—Mix pepper, salt, bread-crumbs, and chopped sage together; rub the head over with butter and put the seasoning upon it; cut the brains in 4 pieces, and rub them also in the crumbs, and lay the head in a deep dish with the brains; put a piece of butter into each eye, with plenty of the crumbs also, fill the dish nearly full of water, and let it bake 2 hours in a quick oven.

———

To Roast a Calf's Head.—Wash and clean it well, parboil it, take out the bones, brains, and tongue; make forcemeat sufficient for the head, and some balls with bread-crumbs, minced suet, parsley, grated ham, and a little pounded veal, or cold owl; season with pepper, salt, grated nutmeg, and lemon peel; bind it with an egg, beaten up, fill the head with it, which must then be sewed up, or fastened with skewers and tied. While roasting, baste it well with butter; beat up the brains with a little cream, the yolk of an egg, some minced parsley, a little pepper and salt; blanch the tongue, cut it into slices, and fry it with the brains, forcemeat balls, and thin slices of bacon. Serve the head with white or brown thickened gravy, and place the tongue, forcemeat balls, and brains round it. Garnish with cut lemon. It will require an hour and a half to roast.

———

Calf's Head Stew.—Parboil the head the day before you want it, and keep the water in which it was boiled for gravy. Cut the meat off the bones the next day in thin slices; fry these in butter or lard, seasoning them with cloves, pepper, salt, sweet marjoram, &c., to your taste. After the slices are fried brown, take them out, and add to the gravy about 1 pint of the liquor in which the head was boiled; thicken with a little brown flour, and put back the slices to stew gently till dinner-time.

Meanwhile have the brains mashed with seasoning as above, add the yolks of 2 eggs beaten, thicken in some flour, and drop them in little pats in the frying pan. Fry them brown and add them to the dish when you serve it. A glass of wine added to the stew just before it is done is to some a great improvement; or a little lemon juice and catsup.

If your family is small, the residue of the head and the liquor in which it was boiled will make soup enough for dinner. For the soup use a small onion, the seasoning above mention ed and allspice. Make dumplings the size of marbles, and cut in quarters 3 or 4 potatoes to boil in it. Calf's head soup should look black from the seasoning and only semi-transparent. The tongue may be used for the stew, or the soup.

———

Calves Brains.—Remove all the large fibres and skin; soak them in warm water for 4 hours; blanch them for 10 minutes in boiling water, with a little salt and vinegar in it; then soak them 3 hours in lemon juice in which a bit of chervil has been steeped; dry them well, dip them in batter, and fry them. Make hot a ladleful of glaze, some extremely small onions browned in butter, artichoke bottoms divided in half, and some mushroom-buttons, and serve round he brains; or, after preparing as above, serve in a rich white acidulated sauce, with lemon juice or tomato sauce.

Or:—Blanch the brains, and beat them up with an egg, pepper, and salt, a small quantity of chopped parsley, and a piece of butter. Make them into small cakes, put them into a small frying-pan, and fry them.

Or:—Prepare them as above; wet with egg, and sprinkle crumbs, salt, pepper, and chopped parsley, and finish dressing in a Dutch oven. Serve with melted butter, with or without a little mushroom catsup.

———

Croquettes of Brains.—Take calf's brains, blanch, and beat them up with 1 or 2 chopped sage leaves, a little pepper and salt, a few bread crumbs soaked in milk, and an egg beaten; roll them into balls, and fry them.

———

Calf's Feet and Ears.—Boil them tender, 3 hours will do, and serve with parsley and butter. Or, having boiled a foot, split it, roll it in bread crumbs, fry it in butter, and serve in brown gravy. Calves' ears may also be dressed as above.

———

Calves' Feet Fricasseed.—Having boiled and split them, as above, simmer them three-quarters of an hour in veal broth, with a blade of mace and lemon peel; and thicken the sauce with flour and butter.

Or:—Soak the feet 3 or 4 hours, and simmer them in milk and water, until the meat can be taken from the bone in handsome pieces; season them with pepper and salt, dip them in yolk of egg, roll in bread crumbs, fry them light brown, and serve in white sauce.

———

Calf's Kidney.—Chop the kidney, and some of the fat, season it with pepper and salt, and make it, with egg and bread crumbs, into balls, which fry in lard or butter; drain upon a sieve, and serve with fried parsley. Or, the lean of cold veal may be substituted for the kidney.

———

Calf's Liver and Lights.—Half boil them, then mince them, and add a little of the water in which they were boiled, with butter and flour to thicken: season with salt and pepper; simmer, and serve hot.

Calf's heart may be stuffed and roasted as beef heart.

———

Calf's Liver and Bacon.—Pare and trim the bacon, and fry it; and, in its fat, fry the liver, in thickish slices, floured. Then lay both in a dish, and pour over them gravy made as follows: Empty the pan, and put into it a small piece of butter, a little broth or water, pepper, salt, and lemon juice; and warm together. Garnish with fried parsley.

———

Veal Forcemeat.—Mix a pound of scraped veal with half the quantity of fat bacon, in a mortar, adding the crumbs of a stale French roll, half a tea-spoonful of powdered nutmeg and mace, a table-spoonful of chopped parsley, and pepper and salt. Mix this well together with 2 well beaten eggs.

———

Egg Balls.—Beat in a mortar 3 hard-boiled yolks of eggs with 1 raw; sprinkle in a little flour and salt, and make the paste into balls.

Both forcemeat and egg balls are much used for savory pies and made dishes.

———

Veal Cake.—Boil six eggs hard, cut them in halves, and lay some of the pieces at the bottom of an earthen pot; then shake in chopped parsley, some slices of veal and ham about two inches square, and then eggs again, repeating the parsley, and seasoning after each layer, until the pot is full. Pour in enough water to cover it, lay about an ounce of butter on the top, tie it over with a thick double paper, and bake it an hour. Press it close together with a spoon, and let it stand till cold. If made in a mould instead of a pot, it forms a handsome supper dish.

MUTTON.

To choose and cook Mutton—Roasted Haunch—Saddle—Loin—Venison Fashion —Shoulder—Leg Braised—Fillet—Breast—To Collar—Boiled Leg—With Oysters—Minced Mutton—Stewed—China Chilo—Cutlets—A la Maintenon— To broil—Rolled Boiled Shoulder—Neck—Horn's Irish Stew—Hotch-Potch— Heart—Kidneys, &c.

No.

1. Leg.
2. Best End of Loin.
3. Chump End of Loin.
4. Neck, Best End.
5. Neck, Scrag End.
6. Shoulder
7. Breast.
A   Saddle is the two Loins.
A   Chine, the two Necks.

To choose Mutton.—The best mutton is small-boned, plump, finely grained, and short-legged; the lean of a dark, rather than of a bright hue, and the fat white and clear: when this is yellow, the meat is rank, and of bad quality. Mutton is not considered by experienced judges to be in perfection until it is nearly or quite five years old; but to avoid the additional expense of feeding the animal so long, it is commonly brought into the market at three years old. The leg and the loin are the superior joints; and the preference would probably be given more frequently to the latter, but for the superabundance of its fat, which renders it a not very economical dish. The haunch consists of the leg and the part of the loin adjoining it; the saddle, of the two loins together, or of the undivided *back* of the sheep: these last are always roasted, and are served usually at good tables, or for company-dinners, instead of the smaller joints. The shoulder, dressed in the ordinary way, is not very highly esteemed, but when boned, rolled, and filled with forcemeat, it is of more presentable appearance, and, to many tastes, far better eating; though some persons prefer it in its natural form, accompanied by stewed onions. It is occasionally boiled or stewed, and covered with rich onion sauce. The neck is sometimes roasted, but it is more generally boiled; the scrag, or that part of it which joins the head, is seldom used for any other purpose than making broth, and should be taken off before the joint is dressed. Cutlets from the thick end of the loin are commonly preferred to any others, but they are frequently taken likewise from the best end of the neck (sometimes called the *back-ribs*) and from the middle of the leg. Mutton kidneys are dressed in various ways, and are excellent in many. The trotters and the head of a sheep may be converted into very good dishes, but they are scarcely worth the trouble which is required to render them palatable. The loin and the leg are occasionally cured and smoked like hams or bacon.

The leg spoils sooner than any other joint of mutton; to prevent which, take out the kernel from the fat, and fill up its place with salt. The neck will keep well, if the pipe be cut out from along the chine-bone. Take out the kernel from the shoulder. Cut the skirt out of the breast. *Lamb* should be managed as mutton. Veal and lamb, it may here be observed, spoil sooner than other meat.

———

Haunch of Mutton Roasted.—It will require to be kept for some time, and must therefore be well washed with vinegar, wiped every day, and, if necessary, rubbed with pounded pepper and ginger.

Cut off the knuckle rather close to the joint of the leg; nick the cramp-bone, and that will allow the cushion or thick part of the leg to draw up and be more plump; trim off the thick skin at the flank, and round off the corner of the fat, so as to make the joint appear neat. Cover the fat with oiled paper, which should be taken off quarter of an hour before you think it will be done; then dredge the meat very lightly with flour, and sprinkle it freely with salt; serve it up with currant jelly and a sauce of port wine, spice, and gravy; a piece of fringed paper being tied neatly around the shank-bone. To roast a haunch of 14 or 16 lbs. will take from 3 to 3½ hours; or even a little more if the weather be very cold, or if required to be "very well done."

To make it taste like Venison.—Let the haunch hang nearly the usual time; then take the skin carefully off, and rub the meat with olive oil, then put it into a pan with a quantity of whole pepper, 4 cloves of garlic, a bundle of sweet herbs, consisting of parsley, thyme, sweet marjoram, and 2 bayleaves. Pour upon the meat a pint of good vinegar and 3 or 4 tablespoonfuls of olive oil. Cover the upper surface of the meat with slices of raw onion, and turn the mutton, every day, always taking care to put the slices of onion on the top surface. At the expiration of 4 days, take the meat out, wipe it with a napkin, and hang it up in a cool place till the next day, when it is fit for roasting.

A more simple method is to rub it every day, and let it hang until it is tender. A clove or two of garlic in the knuckle will, however, give it a much higher flavor, if put into the knuckle when the haunch is hung up.

———

To roast a Saddle of Mutton.—A saddle, *i. e.* the two Loins. being broad, requires a high and strong fire; and, if weighing 11 or 12 pounds, two hours and a half roasting. The skin should be taken off, and loosely skewered on again; or, if this be not done, the fat should be covered with paper, tied on with buttered string. Twenty minutes before the joint is done, take off the skin or paper, baste, flour, and froth it. Serve with gravy and jelly, as haunch of mutton.

A saddle of mutton is an elegant joint, when well trimmed by cutting off the flaps, tail, and chump-end, which will reduce a saddle of 11 pounds to 7 pounds' weight.

———

To Roast a Loin of Mutton.—The flesh of the loin of mutton is superior to that of the leg, when roasted; but to the frugal housekeeper this consideration is usually overbalanced by the great weight of fat attached to it; this, however, when economy is more considered than appearance, may be pared off and melted down for various kitchen uses or finely chopped, and substituted for suet in making hot pie or pudding crust. When thus reduced in size, the mutton will be soon roasted. If it is to be dressed in the usual way, the butcher should be desired to take off the skin; care should be taken to preserve the fat from being ever so slightly burned; it should be managed, indeed, in the same manner as the saddle, in every respect, and carved also in the same way, that is to say, the meat should be cut out in slices the whole length of the backbone, and close to it.

Without the fat, 1 to 1½ hour; with, 1¼ to 1¾ hour.

———

To Dress a Loin of Mutton like Venison.—Skin and bone a loin of mutton, and lay it into a stewpan, or with a pint of water, a large onion stuck with a dozen cloves, half a pint of port wine and a spoonful of vinegar; add, when it boils, a small faggot of thyme and parsley, and some pepper and salt: let it stew three hours, and turn it often. Make some gravy of the bones, and add it at intervals to the mutton when required.

This receipt comes to us so strongly recommended by persons who have partaken frequently of the dish, that we have not thought it needful to prove it ourselves. 3 hours.

———

To Roast a Shoulder of Mutton.—Flour it well, and baste it constantly with its own dripping; do not place it close enough to the fire for the fat to be in the slightest degree burned, or even too deeply browned. An hour and a half will roast it, if it be of moderate size. Stewed onions are often sent to table with it. A shoulder of mutton is sometimes boiled, and smothered with onion sauce.

———

Superior Receipt for Roast Leg of Mutton.—Cover the joint well with cold water, bring it gradually to boil, and let it simmer gently for half an hour; then lift it out, put it immediately on to the spit, and roast it from an hour and a quarter to an hour and a half, according to its weight. This mode of dressing the joint renders it remarkably juicy and tender; but there must be no delay in putting it on the spit after it is lifted from the water; it may be garnished with roast tomatoes, Boiled, half an hour; roast, 1¼ to 1½ hour.

———

Leg of Mutton Braised.—Take a very small leg of mutton, cut off the knuckle, and trim it nicely; half roast it; then put it into a stewpan with the knuckle-bone broken, the trimmings, a few slices of fat bacon or 2 oz. of butter, an onion stuck with cloves, and a bundle of sweet herbs. Shake the stewpan over the fire until there is gravy enough from the meat and the trimmings to stew he mutton, and take care to turn it in the braise. When very tender, take it up, remove the fat from the gravy, strain it, and boil it quickly until it is reduced to a glaze; pour it over the mutton, and serve it up with a purée of vegetables beneath.

———

Fillet of Mutton Roasted.—Cut some inches from either end of a large leg of mutton, and leave the fillet shaped like one of veal. Remove the bone, and fill the cavity with forcemeat made of two cups of bread crumbs and one of butter or minced suet, a little parsley finely shred, the quarter of a nutmeg grated, a tea-spoonful of powdered lemon peel, allspice and salt. Work the whole together with two or three yolks of eggs, well beaten. It may be flavored with a little minced onion, if it is liked: more forcemeat may be added by detaching the skin on the flap side to admit it. Then the fillet may be floured and roasted, served with currant-jelly and brown gravy, or with only melted butter poured over it; or it may be stewed gently for nearly or quite four hours, in a pint of gravy or water, after having been floured and browned all over in a couple of ounces of butter; it must then be turned every hour, that it may be equally done. Two or three small onions, a faggot of herbs, a couple of carrots sliced, four or five cloves, and twenty whole peppercorns can be added at will.

Roasted 2 hours, or stewed 4 hours.

————

Breast of Mutton.—The brisket changes first in the breast: and if it is to be kept, it is best to rub it with a little salt, should the weather be hot.

Cut off the superfluous fat, joint it well, and roast; or to eat cold, sprinkle it well with chopped parsley while roasting.

Or:—Bone it, take off a good deal of the fat, and cover it with bread-crumbs, herbs, and seasoning; then roll and boil till tender: serve with tomato sauce.

Or:—Cut off the fat, and parboil it; take out the bones, and beat the breast flat; season it with pepper and salt; brush it over with the yolk of an egg, and strew over it minced parsley and onions mixed with bread crumbs; baste it well with fresh butter, and broil it. Serve with Sauce Robert.

————

To Collar a Breast of Mutton.—Take out the bone and gristle; then make a forcemeat with bread crumbs, parsley, and sweet herbs, chopped fine, and seasoned with salt and pepper; rub the mutton with yolk of egg, and spread the forcemeat over it, roll it up and tie it tight; and boil 2 hours. If it be eaten hot, make a gravy of the bones, 2 onions, herbs and seasoning, strain, thicken it with butter and flour, and add vinegar and mushroom catsup to flavor; and pour over the mutton. If to be eaten cold, do not remove the tape till the mutton is wanted.

————

Leg of Mutton Boiled.—Let the joint be kept until it is tender, but not so long as for roasting, as mutton for boiling will not look of a good color if it has hung long.

To prepare a leg of mutton for boiling, trim it as for roasting; soak it for a couple of hours in cold water; then put only water enough to cover it, and let it boil gently for 3 hours if of the largest size, and, if smaller, according to its weight. Some cooks boil it in a cloth; but if the water be afterwards wanted for soup, that should not be done, as it would be no longer fit for that purpose: some salt and an onion put into it is far better. When nearly ready, take it from the fire, and, keeping the pot well covered, let it remain in the steam for 10 or 15 minutes. It is sent to table with caper sauce and mashed turnips.

———

To stuff a Leg of Mutton.—Take a leg of mutton, cut off all the fat, take the bone carefully out and preserve the skin whole; take out the meat and mince it fine, and mix and mince with it about 1 lb. of fat bacon and some parsley; season the whole well with pepper and salt, and a small quantity of eschalot or chives chopped fine; then put the meat into the skin and sew it up neatly on the under side; tie it up in a cloth and put it into a stew-pan with 2 or 3 slices of veal, some sliced carrots and onions, a bunch of parsley, and a few slices of fat bacon: let it stew for 3 or 4 hours, and drain the liquor through a fine sieve; when reduced to a glaze, glaze the mutton with it and serve in stewed French beans.

———

To dress a Leg of Mutton with Oysters.—Parboil some fine yell fed oysters, take off the beards and horny parts; put to them some parsley, minced onion, and sweet herbs, boiled and chopped fine, and the yolks of 2 or 3 hard-boiled eggs. Mix all together, and cut 5 or 6 holes in the fleshy part of a leg of mutton, and put in the mixture; and dress it in either of the following ways:—Tie it up in a cloth and let it boil gently for two and a half or three hours, according to the size.

Or:—Braise it, and serve with a pungent brown sauce.

———

Minced Mutton.—Minced dressed meat very finely, season it, make a very good gravy, warm the meat up in it, and serve with fried bread round the dish, or with poached eggs.

———

To Stew a Shoulder of Mutton.—Bone a shoulder of mutton with a sharp knife, and fill the space with the following stuffing:—grated bread, minced suet, parsley, pepper, salt, and nutmeg; bind with the yolks of 2 eggs well beaten. Sew or fasten it with small skewers; brown it in a frying-pan with a bit of butter. Break the bone, put it into a sauce-pan, with some water, an onion, pepper, salt, and a bunch of parsley; let it stew till the strength be extracted; strain, and thicken it with butter rolled in flour; put it, with the mutton, and a glass of port wine, into the sauce-pan; cover it closely, and let it stew gently for two hours. Before serving, add two tablespoonfuls of mushroom catsup. Garnish with pickles.

Or with Oysters.—Hang it some days, then salt it well for two days; bone it, and sprinkle it with pepper and a bit of mace pounded; lay some oysters over it, and roll the meat up tight and tie it; stew it in a small quantity of water, with an onion and a few peppercorns, till quite tender.

Have ready a little good gravy, and some oysters stewed in not, thickened with flour and butter. Take off the tape: pour the gravy over the mutton.

———

To Stew Mutton.—Cut some slices rather thick out of any part of mutton; put them into a stew-pan with some pepper and salt, an onion or two, a sliced carrot, and a little eschalot; cover the steaks with broth, and let them stew from twenty minutes to half an hour, but no longer, or they will become hard; cover the stew-pan close, and when the steaks are about half done, turn them. Before serving, add a little butter rolled in flour, and a spoonful or two of mushroom catsup.

Or:—Cut some slices from an underdone leg of mutton, and put them into a sauce-pan to simmer with half a pint of good gravy, a teaspoonful of white sugar pounded, a small quantity of onion minced, a teacupful of port wine, some pepper and salt, and two or three cloves. This dish should not be allowed to simmer more than five or six minutes.

———

A Camp Dish.—Take any joint of mutton, put it into a pot with a good many onions cut small, and as many vegetables as can be obtained to add to it; 2 tablespoonfuls of vinegar, 5 of port wine; season it with black and red pepper; add a spoonful of flour, and, if at hand, 4 dessert-spoonfuls of Harvey's sauce and essence of anchovies. Cover the meat with water, and let it stew one hour and a half; it should be stirred frequently to prevent it from burning, as there should be only water sufficient to cook it.

———

China Chilo.—Mince a pound of an undressed loin or leg of mutton, with or without a portion of its fat, mix with it two or three young lettuces shred small, a pint of young peas, a teaspoonful of salt, half as much pepper, four tablespoonsful of water, from two to three ounces of good butter, and, if the flavor be liked, a few green onions minced. Keep the whole well stirred with a fork, over a clear and gentle fire until it's quite hot, then place it closely covered by the side of the stove, or on a high trevet, that it may stew as softly as possible for a couple of hours. One or even two half-grown cucumbers, cut small by scoring the ends deeply as they are sliced, or a quarter-pint of minced mushrooms may be added with good effect; or a dessert-spoonful of currie-powder and a large chopped onion. A dish of boiled rice should be sent to table with it.

———

Mutton Cutlets.—Cut the best end of a neck of mutton into cutlets half an inch thick, and chop each bone short; flatten and trim them, scraping the end of the bone quite clean; brush them with egg, and cover them with crumbs, herbs, and, seasoning, and fry them in hot fat; serve them with tomato sauce or any other piquant sauce.

———

With Potato Purée.—The cutlets should be dipped in clarified butter, then in crumbs, afterwards in yolk of egg, and again in crumbs; flatten them with a knife, and fry in hot fat as you would fish. The potatoes are to be boiled, rubbed through a hair-sieve, and worked up fine and light with a little butter and boiling cream; season with pepper, salt, and an atom of nutmeg; dish the cutlets round this purée, which must be softer than mashed potatoes.

———

For Côtelettes de Mouton en Ragoût.—Take off all the fat from the cutlets, dredge the meat with flour, and put them into a stewpan with the fat melted, a bundle of sweet herbs, and 2 shalots minced; let them brown, then strain the gravy, add a glass of wine, or a little lemon-juice, and one of Reading sauce; thicken, if necessary, and let the whole stew until very tender.

———

To dress Côtelette de Mouton à la Polonaise.—Remove all the fat, put the meat into a covered stewpan, with a carrot and a turnip sliced, 2 onions, a bundle of sweet herbs, a little pepper and little pepper and salt, and enough broth to moisten the whole; let it stew very gently until the meat is perfectly done, then take it out, strain the gravy, put it over a brisk fire, and reduce it to a glaze; then cover the cutlets with the glaze, and serve them up with tomato-sauce or a vegetable puree of any kind.

Mutton Cutlets.

For Côtelettes à la Maintenon.—Cut and trim cutlets from a neck or loin of mutton; chop very finely a quantity of parsley a little thyme, and a shalot; put them with butter into a stew pan, and fry the chops a little; then take out the chops; allow them to cool: add to the herbs some fresh parsley chopper and a few crumbs of bread, and seasoning; spread this over the cutlets with a knife, wrap them in buttered paper, and broil them over a slow fire. Serve a sauce piquant in a boat.

Or:—Cut them handsomely from the loin or back end of the neck; half fry them, and then cover them with herbs, crumbs of bread, and seasoning; lay this on very thickly and put them into a stewpan with a little gravy; stew until tender, then wrap them in writing-paper, and finish them on the gridiron.

To broil Mutton Cutlets (Entrée).—These may be taken from the loin, or the best end of the neck, but the former are generally preferred. Trim off a portion of the fat, or the whole of it, unless it be liked; pepper the cutlets, heat the gridiron, rub it with a bit of the mutton suet, broil them over a brisk fire, and turn them often until they are done: this, for the generality of eaters, will be in about 8 minutes if they are not more than half an inch thick, which they should not be. French cooks season them with pepper and salt, and give them a light coating of dissolved butter or of oil, before they are laid to the fire, and we have found the cutlets so managed extremely good.

Lightly broiled, seven or eight minutes. Well done, ten minutes.

Obs.—A cold Mâitre d'Hotel sauce may be laid under the cutlets when they are dished; or they may be served quite dry, or with brown gravy; or when none is at hand, with good melted butter seasoned with mushroom catsup, Cayenne, and Chili vinegar, or lemon juice.

———

Mutton Cutlets stewed in their own Gravy.—Trim the fat entirely from some cutlets taken from the loin; just dip them into cold water, dredge them moderately with pepper, and plentifully on both sides with flour; rinse a thick iron sauce pan with spring-water, and leave a couple of table-spoonsful in it; arrange the cutlets in one flat layer, if it can be done conveniently, and place them over a very gentle fire; throw in a little salt when they begin to stew, and let them simmer as *softly as possible*, but without ceasing, from an hour and a quarter to an hour and a half. If dressed with great care, which they require, they will be equally tender, easy of digestion, and nutritious; and being at the same time free from every thing which can disagree with the most delicate stomach, the receipt will be found a valuable one for invalids. The mutton should be of good quality, but the excellence of the dish mainly depends on its being *most gently stewed;* for if allowed to boil quickly all the gravy will be dried up, and the meat will be unfit for table. The cutlets must be turned when they are half done: a couple of spoonsful of water or gravy may be added to them should they not yield sufficient moisture, but this is rarely needful. From one hour and a quarter to one hour and three-quarters.

Mutton Chops.—Cut the chops off a loin or the best end of a neck of mutton; pare off the fat, dip them in a beaten egg and strew over them grated bread, seasoned with salt and finely-minced parsley; then fry them in a little butter, and make a gravy, or broil them over coals, and butter them in a hot dish. Garnish them with fried parsley.

Rolled Mutton.—Bone a shoulder of mutton carefully, so as not to injure the skin, cut all the meat from the skin, mince it small, and season it highly with pepper, nutmeg, and a clove, some parsley, lemon thyme, sweet marjoram chopped, and a pounded onion, all well mixed, together with a well-beaten yolk of an egg; roll it up very tightly in the skin, tie it round, and bake it in an oven two or three hours, according to the size of the mutton. Make a gravy of the bones and parings, season with an onion, pepper and salt, strain and thicken it with flour and butter; add of vinegar, mushroom catsup, soy, and lemon pickle, a table-spoonful of each, and a tea-cupful of port wine; garnish with forcemeat balls, made of grated bread, and part of the mince.

Shoulder of Mutton, Salted and Boiled.—Bone a shoulder of mutton, if large take 4 oz. of common salt, the same quantity of coarse sugar, mixed with a dessert-spoonful of pounded cloves, half that quantity of pepper, a little pounded mace and ginger; rub them well into the mutton, turning it every day for a week; then roll it up tight, and boil it gently for 3 or 4 hours in a quart of water, with a carrot, turnip, onion, and a bunch of sweet herbs Serve it with some of its own gravy, thickened and highly flavored, or with any piquant sauce; of served up smothered with onions. This is very convenient to families who kill their own mutton. Captains of ships are recommended, when they have fresh mutton, to tow it over board for some hours, and then lay it up in the shrouds. It will then be coated with briny particles which will effectually keep in all the juices.

———

Neck of Mutton.—Is particularly useful, as many dishes may be made of it. The best end of the neck may be boiled for 1½ hour, and served with turnips; or roasted; dressed in steaks; in pies; à-la-Ture; or en haricôt.

The *scrag* may be stewed into broth; or with a small quantity of water, some small onions, a few peppercorns, and a little rice, and served together.

When a neck is to be boiled to look particularly nice, saw down the chine-bone, strip the ribs half-way down, chop off the ends of the bones about 4 inches, and turn the flap under. The skin should not be taken off till boiled, and then the fat will remain white. The neck is very commonly divided, the "scrag" being boiled for broth, and the remaining part either roasted or cut into chops; but, if boiled together, the scrag will require rather more stewing than the other part to make it tender. If only slightly salted, for 2 or 3 days, the fat will be so much improved as to become firm and appear clarified; and the mode which we recommend for dressing the joint is thus:—

Boil the neck very gently until it is nearly done enough; then, ½ an hour or 20 minutes before serving, cover it thickly with bread-crumbs and sweet herbs chopped, with a little drawn butter or the yolk of an egg, and put it into a Dutch oven before the fire. By this process the meat will taste much better than if merely roasted or boiled; the dryness attendant upon roasting will be removed, and the disagreeable greasiness which boiled meat—mutton especially—exhibits, will utterly disappear. Too much cannot be said in favor of this method of dressing the neck and breast of mutton, for the liquor they have been boiled in, if stewed with peas, will make a very good soup.

———

To Harrico a Neck of Mutton.—Roast it till nearly done, then cut it into cutlets, and stew it in a well-seasoned gravy, adding, cut like straws an inch long, the red part of two or three carrots and some turnips.

Irish Stew.—Take two pounds of neck or loin chops; peel and slice two pounds of potatoes, and half a pound of large onions; first put into a stewpan a layer of potatoes, then chops and onions, and so on, till full, sprinkling pepper and salt upon each layer; then pour in cold water or broth, cover the pan, and stew over a very slow fire for an hour and a half, or until the meat be done. Before serving, add two table-spoonsful of mushroom catsup.

———

Hotch-Potch.—Stew peas, onions and carrots, in a very little water, with a beef or ham bone. In the meantime, fry mutton or lamb chops, lean, of a nice brown; then stew them with the vegetables for about half an hour. Serve all together in a tureen.

Hotch-potch may also be made with any two sorts of meat, stewed with vegetables, as above; to which may be added rice, and thickening of butter and flour.

———

Sheep's Tongues.—Boil them till the skin can be taken off; split them, and put them into a stewpan, with some gravy, parsley, mushrooms, and a minced shalot, and some butter pepper, and salt; stew till tender, and strain the gravy over them: or they may be glazed, and served with the gravy under them.

Sheep's tongues may also be skinned, larded, braised, and glazed: and served with onion sauce.

———

Sheep's Heart.—Take a Sheep's Heart and stuff it throughout, using a considerable quantity of chopped bacon in the stuffing; half boil it, and when cooled a little rub it over with pepper and salt, and wrap it in paste in the shape of a cone. Rub the paste over with the yolk of an egg, and strew vermicelli loosely over it. Set it with the broad end downwards and bake it in the oven. When baked, send it to table with gravy sauce.

———

Sheep's Kidney Broiled.—Wash and dry some nice kidneys, cut them in half, and with a small skewer keep them open in imitation of two shells, season them with salt and pepper, and dip them into a little fresh melted butter. Broil first the side that is cut, and be careful not to let the gravy drop in taking them off the gridiron. Serve them in a hot dish, with finely chopped parsley mixed with melted butter, the juice of a lemon, pepper and salt, putting a little upon each kidney.

This is an excellent breakfast for a sportsman.

———

Sheep's Trotters.—Boil the trotters, or rather stew them gently, for several hours, until the bones will come out. The liquor they are boiled in will make excellent stock or jelly. Take out the bones without injury to the skin, stuff them with fine forcemeat; stew them for half an hour in some of the stock, which must be well flavored with onion, seasoning, and a little sauce; take out the trotters, strain the sauce, reduce it to a glaze, and brush it over the feet. Serve with any stewed vegetable.

Or:—Prepare them in the same way, and dip them in a batter and fry them. The paste, or batter, for frying, is best made thus: mix 4 spoonsful of flour with 1 of olive-oil, and a sufficient quantity of beer to make it of the proper thickness; then add the whites of 2 eggs well beaten and a little salt. Serve with tomato-sauce.

Or:—Simply boil them, and eat them cold with oil and vinegar.

———

To send a Leg of Mutton neatly to Table which has been cut for a previous Meal. —Too much must not have been cut from the joint, or it will not answer the purpose. Bone it, cut the meat as a fillet, lay forcemeat inside, roll it, and lay it in a stew-pan with sufficient water to cover it; add various kinds of vegetables, onions, turnips, carrots, parsley, &c., in small quantities; stew two hours; thicken the gravy; serve the fillets with the vegetables round it

LAMB.

To choose and cook Lamb—Saddle, Roasted—To bone Lamb—To stew—Breast,
Loin, Shoulder grilled—To boil a Leg, Neck, or Breast—Lamb's Head—Lamb
Chops—Blanquette d'Agneau—Sweetbread—Fry.

1.   Leg,

2.   Shoulder,

3.   Loin, Best End,

4.   Loin, Chump End,

5.   Neck, Best End,

6.   Breast,

7.   Neck, Scrag End,

NOTE.—A Chine is two Loins: and a Saddle is two Loins, and two Necks of the Best End.

LAMB is a delicate and tender meat; but it requires to be kept a few days, when the weather will permit—and should be thoroughly cooked to be healthful. Never take lamb or veal from the spit till the gravy that drops is white.

The fore-quarter of lamb consists of the shoulder, the neck, and the breast together; the hind-quarter is the leg and loin. There are also the head and pluck, the fry, sweetbreads, skirts, and liver.

In choosing the fore-quarter, the vein in the neck should be ruddy, or of a bluish color. In the hind-quarter, the knuckle should feel stiff, the kidney small, and perfectly fresh. To keep it, the joints should be carefully wiped every day, and in warm weather, sprinkled with a little salt.

The fore quarter is the prime joint, and, if weighing 10 lbs., will require about two hours roasting. In serving, remove the shoulder from the ribs, put between them a lump of butter, sprinkle with pepper and salt, lemon or Seville orange juice; and when the butter is melted, take off the shoulder, and put it into another dish. A hind-quarter, of 8 lbs., will require from one hour and three-quarters to two hours roasting.

A leg of lamb, of 6 lbs., will require an hour and a half roasting.

A shoulder of lamb, an hour.

Ribs, from an hour to an hour and a quarter.

Loin, of 4 lbs., an hour.

Neck, of 3 lbs, three-quarters of an hour.

Breast, three-quarters of an hour.

The gravy for lamb is made as for beef and mutton: it is served with mint sauce; and a joint, to be eaten cold, should be sprinkled with chopped parsley when taken up.

———

To Roast Lamb.—The hind quarter of lamb usually weighs from 7 to 10 pounds: this size will take about two hours to roast it. Have a brisk fire.

It must be very frequently basted while roasting, and sprinkled with a little salt, and dredged all over with flour, about half an hour before it is done.

———

Fore Quarter of Lamb.—A fore quarter of lamb is cooked the same way, but takes rather less time, if the same weight, than the hind quarter; because it is a thinner joint: one of nine pounds ought to be allowed two hours.

———

Leg of Lamb.—A leg of lamb of four pounds' weight will take about an hour and a quarter; if five pounds, nearly one hour and a half; a shoulder of four pounds, will be roasted in an hour, or a very few minutes over.

———

Ribs of Lamb.—Ribs of lamb are thin, and require great care to do gently at first, and brisker as it is finishing, sprinkle it with a little salt, and dredge it slightly with flour, about twenty minutes before it is done. It will take an hour or longer, according to thickness. Gravy for this and other joints of roast lamb, is made as directed elsewhere.

———

Loin, Neck, and Breast of Lamb.—A loin of lamb will be roasted in about an hour and a quarter; a neck in an hour; and a breast in three quarters of an hour. Do not forget to salt and flour these joints about twenty minutes before they are done.

———

Garnish and Vegetables for Roast Lamb.—All joints of roast lamb may be garnished with double parsley, and served up with either asparagus and new potatoes, spring spinach and new potatoes, green peas and new potatoes, or with cauliflowers or French beans and potatoes: and never forget to send up mint sauce.

Obs.—The following will be found an excellent receipt for mint sauce With 3 heaped tablespoonsful of finely-chopped young mint, mix 2 of pounded and sifted sugar, and 6 of the best vinegar: stir it until the sugar is dissolved.

———

To bone a quarter of Lamb.—Take the fore quarter, remove the shoulder, and take out the bone; stuff it with fine forcemeat, and skewer it in a handsome shape. Braise it with 2 oz. of butter, add a teacupful of water, stirring the braise until the gravy is drawn. Then cut the brisket into pieces, and stew them in white gravy; thicken it with cream and eggs so that it shall be very white; cut the long bones into chops and fry them; thicken the gravy of the braise, add to it haricots, minced truffles, or anything else of vegetable in season. Place the shoulder in the centre of a dish with its own sauce, lay the brisket covered with white sauce round it, and place the fried chops at the edge.

———

To Stew Lamb.—A *quarter of lamb* may be stewed by putting it info a stew-pan with a little oil, parsley, chives, and mushrooms, together with some slices of bacon. Let it stew gently in any kind of broth, and when thoroughly done take it out, strain the gravy, and serve the joint along with the mushrooms only. To be well done it will require 4 hours in stewing.

For a Breast of Lamb.—Cut off the thin ends, half boil, then strew with crumbs of bread, pepper and salt, and serve in a dish of stewed mushrooms.

Cut a Loin of Lamb into steaks, pare off the skin and part of the fat, fry it in butter a pale brown, pour away the fat, and put in boiling water enough to cover the meat, a little pepper and salt, a little nutmeg, half a pint of green peas, cover it down, and let it stew gently for half an hour.

———

To stew a Breast of Lamb.—Cut it into pieces, season them with pepper and salt, and stew them in weak gravy: when tender, thicken the sauce, and add a glass of white wine. Cucumbers, sliced and stewed in gravy, may be served with the lamb, the same being poured over it. Or, the lamb may be served in a dish of stewed mushrooms.

———

To Grill a Shoulder of Lamb.—Half-boil it, score it, and cover it with egg, crumbs, and parsley, seasoned as for cutlets. Broil it over a very clear, slow fire, or put it in a Dutch oven to brown it: serve with any sauce that is liked. A breast of lamb is often grilled in the same way.

———

To boil a Leg of Lamb.—This is considered a delicate joint in the very first families. It should be put into a pot with cold water just enough to cover it, and very carefully skimmed so long as the least appearance of scum rises.

This joint should not be suffered to boil fast, for on its being gently boiled depends all its goodness, and the delicate white appearance it should have when served up.

A leg of four or five pounds weight, will take about one hour and a half, reckoning from the time it comes to a boil.

A boiled leg of lamb may be served up with either green peas, or cauliflower, or young French beans, asparagus, or spinach, and potatoes, which for lamb should always be of a small size.

Parsley and butter for the joint, and plain melted butter for the vegetables, are the proper sauces for boiled lamb.

———

To boil a Neck or Breast of Lamb.—Those are small delicate joints, and therefore suited only for a very small family. The neck must be washed in warm water, and all the blood carefully cleaned away.

Either of these joints should be put into cold water, well skimmed, and very gently boiled till done. Half an hour will be about sufficient for either of them, reckoning from the time they come to a boil.

———

To dress Lamb's Head.—Take care that the butcher chops it well through, and cuts out all the nostril bones: when you cook it, take out the brains, lay them into a basin of cold water, and well clean the head in water just milk warm.

When thus cleaned, tie the head up in a sweet clean cloth, and put it into a pot with just enough cold water to cover it. Let it come to a boil very gradually, and take care to remove all the scum as fast as it rises.

It will take about one hour very gentle boiling.

A quarter of an hour before the head is done, pick off the thin black skin from among the brains, wash them clean, tie them up with one or two clean sage leaves in a piece of muslin rag, and let them boil ten minutes.

Then take up the head, just cut out the tongue, skin it, and return it to the head, keeping both warm in the hot cloth and hot water they were boiled in.

Next take up the brains, throw away the sage leaves, and chop up the brains, mixing among them one tablespoonful of parsley and butter, and a small pinch of salt; just give them a gentle warm up in the butter sauce-pan, taking great care they do *not* boil; lay them round the tongue in a small warm dish, and the head in another dish larger and warm.

A sheep's head may be dressed in the same way.

———

Lamb-chops.—Take a loin of lamb, cut chops from it half an inch thick, retaining the kidney in its place; dip them into egg and bread-crumbs, fry and serve with fried parsley.

When chops are made from a breast of lamb, the red bone at the edge of the breast should be cut off, and the breast parboiled in water or broth, with a sliced carrot and 2 or 3 onions, before it is divided into cutlets, which is done by cutting between every second or third bone, and preparing them, in every respect, as the last.

If *house-lamb steaks* are to be done *white*—stew them in milk and water till very tender, with a bit of lemon-peel, a little salt, some pepper and mace. Have ready some veal-gravy, and put the steaks into it; mix some mushroom-powder, a cup of cream, and the least bit of flour; shake the steaks in this liquor, stir it, and let it get quite hot, but not boil. Just before you take it up, put in a few white mushrooms.

If *brown*—season them with pepper, salt, nutmeg, grated lemon-peel, and chopped parsley; but dip them first into egg: fry them quickly. Thicken some gravy with a bit of flour and butter, and add to it a spoonful of port wine.

———

Blanquette d' Agneau. White Fricassee of Lamb.—Cut the best part of the breast of small lamb into square pieces of 2 inches each: wash, dry, and flour them. Having boiled 4 oz. of butter, 1 of fat bacon, and some parsley, 10 minutes, put the meat to it: add the juice of half a lemon, an onion cut small, pepper and salt. Simmer it 2 hours; then add the yolks of 2 eggs, shake the pan over the fire 2 minutes, and serve.

————

Lamb Dressed with Rice.—Half roast a small fore quarter, cut it into steaks; season them with a little salt and pepper; lay them into a dish, and pour in a little water. Boil a pound of rice with a blade or two of mace; strain it, and stir in a good piece of fresh butter, and a little salt, add also the greater part of the yolk of four eggs beaten; cover the lamb with the rice, and with a feather put over it the remainder of the beaten eggs. Bake it in an oven till it has acquired a light brown color.

————

Lamb's Sweetbreads.—Blanch them, and put them into cold water. Then put them into a stewpan, with a ladleful of broth, some pepper and salt, a small bunch of button onions, and a blade of mace: stir in a bit of butter and flour, and stew half an hour. Have ready the yolks of 2 or 3 eggs well beaten in cream, with a little minced parsley and a few grates of nutmeg. Put in some boiled asparagus-tops to the other things. Do not let it boil after the cream is in; but make it hot, and stir it well all the time. Take great care it does not curdle. French beans or peas may be added, but they should be very young.

————

Lamb's Fry.—This is the sweetbreads, skirts, and a portion of the liver. Flour, and season it, and fry plain; or, dip the fry in egg, and strew crumbs over it before frying: serve fried parsley with it, and either of the sauces directed for cutlets. Pork and venison fries are similarly dressed.

VENISON.

To Choose and Cook—Haunch of Venison Roasted—Neck and Shoulder—Venison Steaks—To Stew Venison.

BUCK and Doe Venison are cut up nearly like mutton. The joints are,—

1. Haunch.
2. Neck
3. Shoulder
4. Breast.

The fat should be clear, bright, and thick; and if the cleft of the haunch be smooth and close, it is young; but if the cleft is close and tough, it is old. To judge of its sweetness, run a very sharp narrow knife into the shoulder or haunch, and you will know by the scent. Few people like it when it has much of the *haut-goût;* but it bears keeping better than any sort of meat, and if eaten fresh killed it is not so good as mutton. Observe the neck of a fore-quarter; if the vein be bluish, it is fresh; if it have a green or yellow cast, it is stale. In the hind-quarter, if there is a faint smell under the kidney, and the knuckle is limp, the meat is stale. If the eyes be sunk, the head is not fresh. The haunch is the finest joint. The kernel in the fat, as in the leg of mutton, should be taken out; the part should then be wiped dry, and ground pepper and ginger rubbed on the inside, to keep the flies from it. The neck is the next best joint, and merely requires wiping dry with a clean cloth. The shoulder and breast are mostly used in two or three days for pasties; but sometimes the shoulder is roasted as the haunch.

———

To Roast a Haunch of Venison.—Cut off the knuckle, trim the flap, and remove the thick skin on the flank; nick the joint at the cramp-bone. Spit it, rub it over with butter, sprinkle well with salt, cover it with a sheet of very thin paper, then with a paste of flour and water, and again with paper; tie it up well with a stout string laced across it; baste it all the time it is roasting. Let it cook about 4 or 5 hours. A quarter of an hour before serving it, remove the paste, throw a handful of salt on it, dredge it with flour and baste with a little fresh butter.

The gravy should be made as follows: cut two or three pounds of the scrag, or the lean of a loin of old mutton, brown it on a gridiron, and put it into a saucepan with a quart of water; cover it closely, and simmer for an hour; then uncover it, and stew the gravy to a pint; season *only* with salt, and color brown, and strain.

Another, but much more expensive gravy, is made with a pint of port wine, a pint of strong mutton gravy, as above, and a table-spoonful of currant jelly; let these merely boil up. Or much less wine and more jelly may be used. Seasoned beef gravy is sometimes preferred to mutton gravy.

If the plain gravy only is chosen, cold currant jelly should be erved in a side dish, or boat. Vegetables—French beans and potatoes.

Venison should be served in a metal dish, with a lamp beneath it, else it will soon grow cold.

———

Neck and Shoulder of Venison.—Roast, as the haunch, but with the paste laid on thinner, from two to three hours; and serve as the haunch. A neck is best spitted by putting three skewers through it, and then passing the spit between the skewers and the bones: the top of the ribs should be cut out, and the flap doubled under, as in a neck of mutton for boiling.

Breast of venison may be dressed as above, or baked with mutton gravy, and, when cold, cut up and made into pasty.

Venison, like all wild meats, requires less cooking than tame.

———

Venison Steaks.—Cut them from the neck; season them with pepper and salt. Heat the gridiron well over a bed of bright coals, and grease the bars; lay the steaks on it; broil them well, turning them once, and save as much of the gravy as possible. Serve them with some currant jelly laid on each steak.

———

To Stew cold Venison.—Cut the meat in small slices, and put the trimmings and bones into a saucepan, with barely enough water to cover them. Let them stew 2 hours. Strain the liquor in a stew-pan; add to it some bits of butter rolled in flour, and whatever gravy was left of the venison. Stir in some currant jelly, and let it boil half an hour. Then put in the meat, and keep it over the fire long enough to heat it through, but do not let it boil.

———

A Wet Devil.—Take any part of a turkey, goose, or fowl; cover it with mustard, Chetney, diavolo paste, or any other combustible put a dessert-spoonful of Cayenne pepper, one of pounded white sugar, the juice of a lemon, a glass of wine, and a glass of ketchup, to a tea-cupful of gravy. Heat them together with the deviled fowl, and send up very hot.

N.B. A little cold fresh butter will cool the mouth, should the devil prove too powerful.

PORK.

General Directions—Lard—To roast Pork—Sauce for the Roast—Loin—Head—Shoulder—Chine—Spare-rib—Pork Cutlets—Steaks—Pork Cheese—Pork and Beans—To boil Pork—To cook Pig—Hams—Bacon—Sausages, &c.

1. The Spare Rib,
2. Hand,
3. Belly, or Spring,
4. Fore Loin,
5. Hind Loin
6. Leg.

To choose Pork.—This meat is so proverbially, and we believe even *dangerously* unwholesome when ill fed, or in any degree diseased, that its quality should be closely examined before it is purchased. When not home-fatted, it should be bought, if possible, of some respectable farmer, or miller, unless the butcher who supplies it can be perfectly relied on. Both the fat and lean should be very white, and the latter finely grained; the rind should be thin, smooth, and cool to the touch; if it be clammy, the pork is stale, and should be at once rejected; it ought also to be scrupulously avoided when the fat, instead of being quite clear of all blemish, is full of small kernels, which are indicative of disease.

The manner of cutting up the pork varies in different counties, and also according to the purposes for which it is intended. The legs are either made into hams, or slightly salted for a few days and boiled; they are also sometimes roasted when the pork is not large nor coarse, with a savory forcemeat inserted between the skin and flesh of the knuckle.

The part of the shoulder called the hand, is also occasionally pickled in the same way as hams and bacon, or it may be salted and boiled, but it is too sinewy for roasting. After these and the head have been taken off, the remainder, without further division than being split down the back, may be converted into whole sides or *flitches*, as they are usually called, of bacon; but when the meat is large, and required in part for various other purposes, a chine may be taken out, and the fat pared off the bones of the ribs and loins for bacon; the thin part of the body converted into pickled pork, and the ribs and other bones roasted, or made into pies or sausages. The feet, which are generally salted down for immediate use, are excellent if laid for two or three weeks into the same pickle as the hams, then well covered with cold water, and slowly boiled until tender.

The loins of young and delicate pork are roasted with the skin on; and this is scored in regular stripes of about a quarter of an inch wide with the point of a sharp knife, before the joints are laid to the fire. The skin of the leg also is just cut through in the same manner. This is done to prevent its blistering, and to render it more easy to carve, as the skin *(or crackling)* becomes so crisp and hard in the cooking, that it is otherwise sometimes difficult to divide it.

To be at any time fit for table, pork must be perfectly sweet, and thoroughly cooked; great attention also should be given to it when it is in pickle, for if any part of it be long exposed to the air, without being turned into, or well and frequently basted with the brine, it will often become tainted during the process of curing it.

———

To Melt Lard.—Strip the skin from the inside fat of a freshly killed and well-fed pig; slice it small and thin; put it into a new or well-scalded jar, set it into a pan of boiling water, and let it simmer over a clear fire. As it dissolves, strain it into small stone jars, or deep earthen pans, and when perfectly cold, tie over it the skin that was cleared from the lard, or bladders which have been thoroughly washed and wiped very dry. Lard thus prepared is extremely pure in flavor, and keeps perfectly well, if stored in a cool place; it may be used with advantage in making pastry, as well as for frying fish, and for various other purposes. It is better to keep the last drainings of the fat apart from that which is first poured off, as it will not be quite so fine in quality.

———

To Preserve Unmelted Lard for many months.—It may be kept well during the summer months by rubbing fine salt rather plentifully upon in when it is first taken from the pig, and leaving it for a couple of days; it should then be well drained, and covered with a strong brine: this, in warmer weather, should be changed occasionally. When wanted for use, lay it into cold water for two or three hours, then wipe it dry, and it will have quite the effect of the fresh leaf when made into paste.

Inner fat of pig, 6 lbs.; fine salt, ½ to ¾ lb.: 2 days. Brine, to each quart of water, 6 ozs. salt.

———

To roast a Leg of Pork.—Cut a slit near the knuckle, and fill the space with sage and onion, chopped fine, and seasoned with pepper and salt, with or without bread-crumbs. Rub sweet oil on the skin, to prevent it blistering and make the crackling crisp; and the outer rind may be scored with lines, about half an inch apart. If the leg weigh seven or eight pounds, it will require from two and a half to three hours' roasting before a strong fire. Serve with apple-sauce and potatoes; which are likewise eaten with all joints of roasted pork.

If the stuffing be liked mild, scald the onions before chop ping them.

If pork is not stuffed, you may serve it up with sage and onion sauce, as well as apple-sauce, which should always accompany roast pork, whether it is stuffed or not; and also with mustard.

Roast leg of pork must always be served up with plenty of nicely boiled potatoes.

———

To make Sage and Onion sauce.—Chop fine as much green sage leaves as will fill a dessert-spoon after they are chopped, and chop as much onion very fine as will fill a table-spoon after it is chopped, and let them simmer gently in a butter saucepan, with four table-spoonsful of water, for ten minutes; then add half a tea-spoonful of pepper, half a tea-spoonful of salt, and one ounce of grated bread crumbs: when these are well mixed pour to them a quarter of a pint of thin melted butter, or as much gravy, and let the sauce simmer a few minutes, stirring it all the time, and serve it up hot in a sauce tureen.

———

To make Apple-sauce.—Pare, quarter, and core five or six large apples into a saucepan, with three table-spoonsful of water, cover the saucepan close, and place it over a slow fire two hours before you want the sauce. When the apples are done quite soft, pour off the water, and beat them up with a piece of butter the size of a nutmeg, and a dessert-spoonful of powdered lump-sugar. The apples must be tried while they are stewing, to know when they are quite soft; for some kinds of apples will take a longer time than others. Some persons use moist sugar.

The Spring, or Fore-loin of Pork.—Cut out the bone, and, in its place, put a stuffing of sage and onion, made as directed for roast pork. Skewer it in the joint; hang it down to a moderate fire, and allow it about twenty minutes to a pound; but you must give a little more or less time, according to its thickness, more than to its weight: only do it slowly till rather more than half done; and finish it off with a brisker fire. Serve it up with potatoes and apple sauce; same as the leg.

Loin and Neck of Pork.—Simmer the best end of either of the joints till nearly fit for the table, strip off the skin, put it into a cradle-spit, wet it all over with yolks of eggs, and cover it thickly with crumbs of bread, sweet herbs and chives chopped fine for stuffing, and seasoned with pepper and salt. It will get a good brown in about half an hour.

Either of them may also be *rolled.*—Bone it: put a forcemeat of chopped sage, a very few crumbs of bread, salt, pepper, and two or three berries of allspice, over the inside; then roll the meat as tight as you can, and roast it slowly, and at a good distance at first from the fire.

To parboil it before the herbs are put on will be an improvement.

A hand of pork may likewise be boned, stuffed, rolled, and roasted, as above.

To roast a Porker's Head.—Clean it, and take out the eyes and snout; stuff it with sage and bread crumbs, seasoned, sew it up firmly, and roast it before a quick fire, or bake it.

Pig's head may be stuffed as above, or with onions, and baked.

Belly of Pork.—Lovers of pork are very fond of having the belly part of a porker, either fresh or salted, strewed thickly over the inside with sage, sweet herbs, and minced eschalots, then rolled, tied tightly together, and either baked or roasted.

Shoulders and Breasts of Pork.—Put them into pickle, or salt the shoulder as a ham; cut accordingly. When very nice, they may be roasted.

Chine of Pork.—The chine is more usually salted, and served as an accompaniment to roast turkey. Salt the chine for three days, roast it, and serve it up with sauce made thus: Fry in oil or butter two or three sliced onions until they take color; then pour off the oil, and add some gravy-sauce, chopped mushrooms, and two tablespoonfuls of vinegar, with one teaspoonful of made mustard. Give the whole a boil, and serve it up in the dish.

———

To roast a Spare-rib of Pork.—A spare-rib of 8 or 9 lbs. weight will require from 2 to 3 hours roasting; though the time depends more upon the thickness than the weight: if it be very thin, it will be done in half the above time. On putting it down, baste it with a little butter; and, about 20 minutes before it is done, dry a few sage leaves, rub them to powder, mix salt and pepper with them, and sprinkle over the pork.

———

The *griskin* may be roasted as above: if of 7 or 8 lbs. weight, it will require an hour and a half.

———

To broil or fry Pork Cutlets.—Cut them about half an inch thick from a delicate loin of pork, trim them into neat form, and take off part of the fat, or the whole of it when it is not liked; dredge a little pepper or Cayenne upon them, and broil them over a clear and moderate fire from 15 to 18 minutes, sprinkle a little fine salt upon them just before they are dished. They may be dipped into egg and then into bread, crumbs mixed with minced sage, then finished in the usual way. When fried, flour them well, and season them with salt and pepper first. Serve them with gravy made in the pan, or with sauce Robert.

———

Pork Cutlets and Tomato Sauce.—Cut the bone out of pork chops, and trim off part of the fat, fry them delicately, and drain them; then simmer them a few minutes in a stew-pan with tomato sauce, made as follows:—Chop a shalot very fine; put it into a small stew-pan, with a little vinegar, simmer, and add some tomato sauce, with brown gravy, to taste: dish the chops with the sauce in the middle, and round them. Or, the cutlets may be fried with bread crumbs, and served upon tomato sauce.

———

Blade-bone of Pork.—Broil it, and when done, pepper and salt it; rub over it a piece of butter, and serve very hot.

———

Pork Steaks.—Cut them off a neck or loin; trim them neatly, and pepper them; broil them over a clear fire, turning them frequently; they will take 20 minutes. Sprinkle with salt when put in the plate, and add a small piece of butter.

———

Italian Pork Cheese.—Chop, not very fine, 1 lb. of lean pork with 2 lbs. of the inside fat; strew over and mix thoroughly with them 3 tea-spoonsful of salt, nearly half as much pepper, a half-tea-spoonful of mixed parsley, thyme, and sage (and sweet basil, if it can be procured), all minced extremely small. Press the meat closely and evenly into a shallow tin, and bake it in a very gentle oven from an hour to an hour and a half: it is served cold, in slices. Should the proportion of fat be considered too much, it can be diminished on a second trial.

———

Pork and Beans is an economical dish, but it does not agree with weak stomachs. Put a quart of beans into two quarts of cold water, and let them stand all night near the fire. In the morning, pour off the water, rinse them well with two or three waters poured over them in a colander. Take a pound of rather lean pork, salted, score the rind, then place the beans just covered with water in the kettle, and keep them hot an hour or two; then drain off the water, sprinkle a little pepper and a teaspoonful of salt over the beans: place them in a well glazed earthen pot, not very wide at the top, put the pork down in the beans, till the rind only appears; fill the pot with water till it just reaches the top of the beans; put it in a brisk over and bake three or four hours.

Stewed beans and pork are prepared the same way, only they are kept over the fire for three or four hours instead of in the oven.

———

To Boil a Leg of Pork.—Pickled pork takes more time to boil than other meat. If you buy your pork ready salted, ask how many days it has been in salt; if many, it will require to be soaked in water before you dress it. When you cook it, wash and scrape it as clean as possible; when delicately dressed, it is a favorite dish with almost every body. Take care it does not boil fast; if it does, the knuckle will break to pieces, before the thick part of the meat is warm through; a leg of seven pounds takes three hours and a half very slow simmering. Skim your pot very carefully, and do not allow any scum to settle on the meat. The proper vegetables are parsnips, potatoes, turnips, or carrots. Some like cabbage; but it is a strong, rank vegetable, and does not agree with a delicate stomach. It should not be given to children.

———

Pork Cheeks.—Divide the head, clean it, and take away the snout, eyes, and brains. Salt it with common salt and salt-petre for eight or ten days, when it will be fit to boil for two hours. Or, the cheek may be salted only three or four days, and then washed, and simmered with peas till tender.

———

Sucking-Pigs: to Scald a Sucking-Pig.—The moment the pig is killed, put it into cold water for a few minutes; then rub it over with a little resin, beaten extremely small, and put it into a pail of scalding water half a minute; take it out, lay it on a table, and pull off the hair as quickly as possible: if any part does not come off, put it on again. When quite clean, wash it with warm water, and then in two or three cold waters, that no flavor of the resin may remain. Take off the feet at the first joint; make a slit down the belly and take out the entrails: put the liver, heart, and lights, to the feet. Wash the pig well in cold water, dry it thoroughly, and fold it in a wet cloth to keep it from the air.

———

Roast Pig.—A sucking pig is nicest when about three weeks old; and should, if possible, be dressed the same day it is killed; one of this age will take about two hours to roast.

The most particular thing in dressing a sucking pig is carefully to cleanse thoroughly; to do which you must take the wax out of the ears, and the dirt from the nostrils, by using a small skewer covered with a bit of thin rag, which you must wipe off upon a clean dish-cloth; then take out the eyes with a fork or a sharp-pointed knife, clean the tongue, gums, and lips, by scraping them with a clean knife, and wiping them, being careful not to cut them, and with your hand up the inside of the throat, take out all the clotted blood and loose pieces you will find there; and lastly, you must cleanse the other end of the pig also most carefully, by putting a thick skewer covered with a piece of rag through from the inside, so as to push every thing out at the tail, which generally comes out with a small portion of the pipe with it, wiping the inside of the pig clean with a damp cloth; and unless all this is done by the cook, a sucking pig cannot be very nice; and for want of knowing how to do it, they are frequently brought to table not far from offensive: for butchers and porkmen never do clean them properly, whatever they may tell you, or promise you.

When all this is done, and the stuffing sewed into the belly, (to make which, see the two following receipts,) wipe the outside of the pig, and rub it well all over with a table-spoonful of salad oil or fresh butter, (but oil is the best,) cover the loins with a piece of greased writing-paper, and hang it down to a pretty good fire, giving most of the heat to the rump and shoulders, as they require more doing than the loin part; therefore, when the loin is done enough, put the ends to the fire to finish them. While it is roasting, you must based it well, very frequently, with nice sweet dripping, to keep the skin from blistering, till within about 20 minutes of its being done, when you must take the paper off, and baste it with a little butter.

When you serve up the pig, the two sides must be laid back to back in the dish, with half the head on each side, and one ear at each end, all with the crackling side upwards. Garnish the dish with slices of lemon; and serve it up with rich gravy in one sauce-tureen, and with brain sauce, or bread sauce, in another.

To make Stuffing for a Sucking-Pig.—Chop fine or crumble two dozen good-sized clean sage leaves, four ounces of stale crumb of bread grated, and one ounce of butter, broken into small pieces; mix them well together with a tea spoonful of pepper, and half as much salt; put all into the belly of the pig, and sew it up.

Another way to make Stuffing for a Pig.—Chop fine or crumble two dozen good sized clean sage leaves, and mix them with half a small salt-spoonful of cayenne pepper, half a tea spoonful of pepper, and half a tea-spoonful of salt; then cut four slices of crumb of bread and butter, about four inches long, two wide, and a quarter of an inch thick; roll the bread and butter in the herbs and seasoning, and put them into the pig, and sew it up.

To make Brain Sauce.—Before the pig is served up, put it into a dish, cut off the head, and cut the pig down the middle into two parts; then cut off the ears, and cut the head in two, take out the brains, chop them very fine with about a tablespoonful of the stuffing taken from the inside of the pig, and all the gravy which runs from the pig when it is cut; put it all into a saucepan, with a large table-spoonful of melted butter, give it a warm up, stirring it all the time, and send it up in a sauce tureen.

———

To Bake a Sucking-Pig.—A sucking-pig is one of the few things which is rather nicer baked than roasted. You must clean and stuff it, and prepare it exactly the same as for roasting, except that you must mix the yolk of a raw egg with the table-spoonful of salad-oil, and rub it well all over the pig; cover the ears with well buttered paper; allow two or three ounces of butter, to baste it with. For a baked pig, you must make gravy, and sauce, and send it to table in every thing the same as directed for roast pig.

It takes about two hours to bake.

———

To Choose and Boil Ham.—Stick a sharp knife under the bone, and also up to the knuckle. If it comes out with a pleasant smell, the ham is good; but do not buy it if the knife has a bad scent. Hams short in the hock are best; nor should long-legged pigs be chosen for any purpose.

If the rind be thin, the fat firm and of a reddish tinge, the lean tender, of a good color, and adhering to the bone, you may conclude it is good and not old. If there are yellow streaks in it, it is rusty.

All hams require soaking and scraping before they are dressed, to make them clean and tender. An old dry ham should be laid to steep in cold water about twenty-four hours; though half that time may be enough for a small ham, or one that is not very dry. When the ham has steeped long enough, take it out of the water, cut off all the ragged, rusty, or decayed parts, from the sides and under part, and make it perfectly clean all over, by a nice and careful scraping. Put it into a pot with enough cold water completely to cover it about two inches, but not more, and let it be heated slowly, so that it may be an hour and a half to two hours before it begins to boil. It must be well skimmed so long as any scum will arise, and then covered close down and kept simmering very gently till it is done. From four to five hours gently boiling will in general be enough for a ham that weighs fifteen or sixteen pounds, reckoning from the time it comes to a boil, but allowances must be made for the thickness or thinness of the ham, and for the time it has been kept. If the ham is thin, you must allow rather less time.

When the ham is done, the skin should be carefully peeled off, without breaking, if possible, as it will serve to cover the ham, and keep it moist, when it is put by. As soon as you have pulled off the skin, coat the top of the ham over with brown raspings, by rasping over it a little of the crust from the bottom side of a loaf. Then trim and wipe the knuckle, and wrap round it a piece of writing paper, fringed, to hold it by in carving.

The dish may be garnished with either thin slices of turnips or carrots, or slices of lemon.

If the ham is not to be cut till it is cold, it should be allowed to boil gently half an hour longer than if it is intended to be cut while hot.

———

Another Way.—We have seen the following manner of boiling a ham recommended, but we have not tried it:—"Put into the water in which it is to be boiled, a quart of old cider and a pint of vinegar, a large bunch of sweet herbs, and a bay-leaf. When it is two-thirds done, skin, cover it with raspings, and set it in an oven until it is done enough: it will prove incomparably superior to a ham boiled in the usual way."

A good Flavoring for Gravies and soups.—The gravy which runs out of ham when it is cut, is called essence of ham, and should be very carefully saved to flavor soups or gravies.

———

French Receipt for Boiling a Ham—After having soaked, thoroughly cleaned, and trimmed the ham, put over it a little very sweet clean hay, and tie it up in a thin cloth; place it in a ham kettle, a braising pan, or any other vessel as nearly of its size as can be, and cover it with two parts of cold water, and one of light white wine (we think the reader will perhaps find *cider*, a good substitute for this); add, when it boils and has been skimmed, four or five carrots, two or three onions, a large bunch of savory herbs, and the smallest bit of garlic. Let the whole simmer gently from four to five hours, or longer should the ham be very large. When perfectly tender, lift it out, take off the rind, and sprinkle over it some fine crumbs, or some raspings of bread mixed with a little finely minced parsley.

———

To Bake a Ham.—Unless when too salt, from not being sufficiently soaked, a ham (particularly a young and fresh one) eats much better baked than boiled, and remains longer good. The safer plan is to lay it into plenty of cold water over night. The following day soak it for an hour or more in warm water, wash it delicately clean, trim smoothly off all rusty parts, and lay it with the rind downwards into a coarse paste rolled to about an inch thick; moisten the edges, draw, pinch them together, and fold them over on the upper side of the ham, taking care to close them so that no gravy can escape. Send it to a well-heated, but not a fierce oven. A very small ham will require three hours baking, and a large one five. The crust and the skin must be removed while it is hot. When part only of a ham is dressed, this mode is better far than boiling it.

———

Ham Relish.—Cut a slice of dressed ham, season it highly with Cayenne-pepper, and broil it brown; then spread mustard over it, squeeze on it a little lemon juice, and serve quickly.

———

Broiled Ham.—Cut ham into thin slices, and broil on a gridiron. If the ham is too salt, soak the slices before broiling, in cold water; if you are obliged to do this, dry them well whom a cloth before broiling.

Fry what eggs you want in butter, and when dished lay an egg on each slice of ham, and serve.

———

Fried Ham and Eggs.—Broil thin slices of ham; fry eggs in the gravy of the ham or in butter, and serve one on each slice of ham. Or, the eggs may be poached.

———

Sausages.—Common farm-house sausages are made with nearly equal parts of fat and lean pork, coarsely chopped, and seasoned with salt and pepper only. They are put into skins (which have previously been turned inside out, scraped very thin, washed with exceeding nicety, and wiped very dry) then twisted into links, and should be hung in a cool airy larder, when they will remain good for some length of time. Odd scraps and trimmings of pork are usually taken for sausage meat when the pig is killed and cut up at home; but the chine and blade-bone are preferred in general for the purpose. The pork rinds will make a strong and almost flavorless jelly, which may be used with excellent effect for stock, and which, with the addition of some pork-bones, plenty of vegetables, and some dried peas, will made a very nutritious soup for those who do not object to the pork-flavor which the bones will give. Half an ounce of salt, and nearly or quite a quarter of an ounce of pepper will sufficiently season each pound of the sausage-meat.

———

Excellent Sausages.—Chop, first separately, and then together, one pound and a quarter of veal, perfectly free from fat, skin, and sinew, an equal weight of lean pork, and of the inside fat of the pig. Mix well, and strew over the meat an ounce and a quarter of salt, half an ounce of pepper, one nutmeg grated, and a large tea-spoonful of pounded mace. Turn, and chop the sausages until they are equally seasoned throughout, and tolerably fine; press them into a clean pan, and keep them in a very cool place. Form them, when wanted for table, into cakes something less than an inch thick, flour and fry them for about 10 minutes in a little butter.

Lean of veal and pork, of each, 1 lb. 4 oz.; fat of pork, 1 lb. 4 oz.; salt, 1¼ oz.; pepper, ½ oz.; 1 nutmeg; 1 large tea spoonful of mace. Fried in cakes, 10 minutes.

Oxford Sausages.—Chop a pound and a half of lean pork very finely, and mix with it half the quantity of minced beef-suet; add 2 or 3 table-spoonsful of bread crumbs, the yolks of 2 eggs, beaten, and season with dried sage, black pepper, and salt; beat the whole well together in a marble mortar, put it into a jar, and tie over. For use, make it into rolls, dust them with flour, and fry in lard, or fresh beef-dripping.

———

To fry Sausages.—Put lard or dripping, into a clean frying pan, and as soon as it is melted, put in the sausages, fry them gradually over a moderate fire, shaking the pan and turning them frequently. When done, put them before the fire on a sieve, to drain off the fat, and serve hot.

———

Bologna Sausages.—Mince 6 lbs. of rump of beef very fine, and 2 lbs. of bacon; pound them; mix well with 6 or 8 cloves of garlic; season it high with spices; fill it into very large hog-puddings, and tie them in 9 inch lengths; hang them in a dry, warm place, or in the smoke: they are eaten raw or boiled.

———

To dress Pig's Feet and Ears.—Boil them, fresh or salted, 3 hours, or till tender, when take out the large bones; glaze them, and cover them with fried bread crumbs, and serve upon tomato sauce: or, melted butter thinned with mustard and vinegar.

———

To stew Pig's Feet.—Clean and split them, and boil them tender; then put them into a stew-pan, with a little gravy or water, a shred onion, sage leaves, salt, some whole black pepper, and allspice: stew for half an hour: then strain the gravy, thicken it with butter and flour, add a table-spoonful of lemon pickle, or vinegar, and serve with the feet.

———

Pig's Harslet.—Clean the liver and sweetbreads, and put to them fat and lean bits of pork, with which mix pepper, salt, sage, and onions shred fine: put all into a caul, tie up, and roast on a hanging-jack; or put into a dish and bake.

Or:—Slice the liver and sweetbreads, and fry them with pieces of bacon; garnish with fried parsley.

American Souse.—Take pig's feet and ears, &c.; clean them well, and simmer them for 4 or 5 hours, until they are too tender to be taken out with a fork. Then lay them in cold water till they are cool. Pack them down tight in jars. Boil the jelly-like liquor in which they were cooked, with an equal quantity of vinegar, and salt to your taste: add cloves, allspice and cinnamon, and pour it over the feet.